THE LION
Children's Bible

Stories from the Old and New Testaments
retold by Pat Alexander

Illustrated by Lyndon Evans

SANDY
LANE
BOOKS

Copyright © 1981 Lion Publishing

Published by
Sandy Lane Books
Sandy Lane West, Oxford, England
ISBN 0 7459 4000 5
Albatross Books Pty Ltd
PO Box 320, Sutherland, NSW 2232, Australia
ISBN 0 7324 1346 X

This edition 1995
10 9 8 7 6 5 4 3 2 1 0

Text by Pat Alexander
Illustrations by Lyndon Evans

The author asserts the moral right
to be identified as author of this work

A catalogue record for this title
is available from the British Library

Printed and bound in Malaysia

Contents

The story of God's people
THE OLD TESTAMENT

The story of Jesus and his followers
THE NEW TESTAMENT

The story of God's people

THE OLD TESTAMENT

We begin at the very beginning,
before the world itself was made.
In the beginning there was God.
He made the world and everything in it.
He made the first people.
And when things began to go wrong,
God planned a way out.
He chose one man,
and through him a nation,
and from that nation a Saviour.
The Bible contains a marvellous collection
of stories.
It is also one story . . .

In the beginning

Long ago, when things began, God made our world. He made the sun to light the day. He made the moon and stars for the night. He made the sky and land and sea.

He made birds to fly in the sky, fish to swim in the sea, and animals for the land. God looked around at all that he had made, and he was very pleased. The world was ready for people. So God made a man and a woman—Adam and Eve.

God put Adam and Eve in charge of his new world—to look after the plants and trees, the birds and fish and animals. He gave them a lovely place to live in. There were cool rivers, shady trees, and all kinds of fruit to eat. The place was called the garden of Eden.

Adam and Eve were very happy. There was just one thing that God told them they must never do. They were not to eat the fruit of one special tree—the tree of the knowledge of good and evil. If they did, God said they would die. So Adam and Eve lived as God's friends. And did as he said.

But there was someone who wanted to spoil God's world. One day, as Eve was walking past the special tree— the tree of the knowledge of good and evil—she heard the soft, hissing voice of the snake.

'See how good this fruit is. Doesn't it make your mouth water? Why not try it? The fruit will make you wise. If you eat it you will be as clever as God is.'

Eve listened to the snake's soft voice. She looked at

the fruit. And she forgot how good and kind God was. She wanted to be as clever as God. She wanted to do as she liked.

Eve stretched out her hand and picked the fruit. She began to eat—and she gave some to Adam.

From that moment things began to go wrong.

God knew what Adam and Eve had done. No one can hide anything from him. Adam and Eve weren't God's friends any more, and he sent them away.

They had to leave the garden of Eden, where they had been so happy, where they had walked and talked with God. An angel with a sword stood guard to stop them ever coming back.

Now they had to work hard, so hard that they ached with tiredness. They learnt what pain felt like. But worst of all, God's dreadful warning came true: they knew that when they grew old, they would die.

After they left the garden of Eden, Adam and Eve had two sons: Cain and Abel. When they grew up, Cain became a farmer, digging the soil and planting his crops. Abel looked after his father's flocks. He was a shepherd.

At harvest time Cain brought some of his crops and gave them as a present to God. It was his way of saying thank you. Abel gave God one of his lambs. They were good presents. But we can't buy God's love with presents. He looks to see what kind of people we are.

Abel was a good man, so God was pleased with Abel's present. But Cain was jealous and angry. He hated his brother Abel. And he knew that God was not pleased with his present.

One day, out in the fields, Cain killed Abel. He thought no one had seen him. But God knew what he had done.

God punished Cain by sending him away from his home and family for ever. God's new world, the world that was so good, was already being spoilt.

Noah's boat

A long time passed. People were born. They had
children. They died. And all the time things were going
from bad to worse in God's world. People fought one
another. They hated and hurt one another. They did
not care about God, or the way he wanted them to live.
No one listened to him any more—and God began to be
sorry he had ever made man. There was only one thing
to do. He must make a fresh start with new people.
Sadly, he decided to destroy every living creature on the
earth. He decided to send a great flood.

But there was one good man who lived as God's
friend. His name was Noah. God talked to Noah about
the flood, and explained his plan. He wanted to save
Noah and his family. God told Noah to build a great
boat. It must be big enough for Noah and his wife, their
three sons, Ham, Shem and Japheth with their wives,
and two of every kind of animal and bird. And there
had to be room to store food to feed them all for a very
long time. Noah listened carefully, and did exactly as
God said.

People came to watch him work on the boat—it was
a long job. Every day when they asked him what he was
doing he told them what God had said about the flood.
But they took no notice. They thought Noah was
crazy. He must be. Fancy building a boat on dry land,
miles from a river or sea! But Noah did not let them

stop him. He got on with the work and at last the boat was finished.

Then the rain came.

That day Noah and his family and all the birds and animals went into the boat, as God had said. And God shut the door tight behind them.

The rain came down in torrents. And it kept on raining, day after day. Soon all the rivers overflowed and the water spread over the ground. It reached the boat. It swirled around, growing deeper and deeper. Then it lifted the boat, and Noah and all his family were afloat.

Still the rain came and the water rose and rose until everything was covered. No one, nothing survived. Not even the tops of the mountains could be seen. Noah and his family, and the animals with them in the boat, were the only ones left alive. It was an empty, lonely world.

At last the rain stopped. Slowly, slowly the water began to go down, until the boat came to rest among the mountains. Noah wanted to find out if the earth was dry enough for everyone to leave the boat. So he opened a window and let out a raven. When the raven did not come back, Noah let out a dove. But it was not yet dry enough for the dove, so she flew back, and Noah let her in again.

The next time the dove flew out she brought back a fresh green leaf from an olive-tree. Then Noah knew that the earth was nearly dry. The third time the dove flew out, she did not return. Soon Noah could see the dry land for himself.

Then God told Noah it was time for them all to leave the boat and make a fresh start in the clean, new world. What an exciting day that was! Animals and people tumbled over one another in the rush to get out of the boat and stand on dry land again. Noah and his family laughed and shouted, and ran about. Then they thanked God for keeping them safe.

They built up a heap of big stones and put wood on top, to make an 'altar' where they could roast meat as a special thank-you present to God. And, as the sun broke through, overhead, across the sky, arched a beautiful rainbow. For God had promised Noah that he would never again send a flood to destroy the earth. And the rainbow was a sign, for everyone to see, that he would keep his promise for ever and ever.

The Tower of Babel

After the great flood, Noah and his sons farmed the land and planted vines. They had children, and their children had children. Soon there were so many people that some families had to move away to find fresh grass for their animals to graze.

But still they all spoke the same simple language and everyone could understand one another. It was easy for them to plan and work together.

Some of them settled in the plains of Babylonia. They learnt to make bricks and bake them hard to make them strong. They discovered how to use tar to hold them together. Now they could really build!

One day someone said, 'Let's build ourselves a city. And let's make a great tower, the tallest that has ever been built. Then we'll be famous.' Everyone agreed that this was a good idea, and soon they were all hard at work. They began to build the Tower of Babel.

God watched them at work. He saw the walls growing higher and higher. He saw the people getting bigger and bigger ideas. And he knew that this would lead to trouble. Men were beginning to think they could do anything. They were beginning to think they were gods.

So God did not wait till the tower was finished. If people spoke different languages they would not be able to understand one another. It would be more difficult to work together. So God mixed up their languages and scattered the people to different parts of the world.

North, south, east and west they went. Some settled on the coasts and islands at the eastern end of the

Mediterranean Sea. Some made their homes in Egypt and Africa. Others went to Assyria and Arabia.

The families descended from Noah grew into great nations, each in its own country. And every nation spoke a different language. Never again were they able to work and plan together so easily. And whenever people talked of the great Tower of Babel, they remembered how it was that men came to speak a 'babble' of different languages.

Abraham and Lot

In the city of Ur, in the country of Chaldea, there lived a man called Abraham. His wife's name was Sarah. One day God said to Abraham:

'I want you to leave Ur and go far away to the country of Canaan. If you do as I say, I will make you the father of a great nation.'

Now Abraham and Sarah had no children. But they believed God and did as he said. They took Lot, Abraham's nephew, and their servants, their flocks and their herds, and they left Ur. They left their family and home and friends—all the people and places they knew so well—and set out for an unknown land.

Travel was slow, and the journey to Canaan a long one, but at last they arrived. They set up their tents at Mamre, near Hebron, and for a long time they all lived happily together. But as the herds of cattle and flocks of sheep increased there was not enough water or grass for them all. There were quarrels between the men who looked after Abraham's cattle and the men who looked after Lot's.

So Abraham and Lot decided it was time to part. Abraham let Lot choose where he wanted to go. Lot decided to move down from the hills into the green valley of the River Jordan close to the town of Sodom. There he would have plenty of water and good grass for his flocks. Lot moved off. This meant that Abraham had to stay up on the hills, where there wasn't much water and the grass was thin and brown.

But although the valley looked good, Lot had made the wrong choice. The people who lived in Sodom were proud and greedy and lazy; they were hard, cruel and violent. Terrible things were done in Sodom and no one was sorry or ashamed.

But God is just. He will not turn a blind eye to those who deliberately do wrong. The city of Sodom deserved to be punished.

One hot midday, when Abraham was resting in the shade of his tent, he saw three strangers coming towards him. He went to greet them and invited them to rest and eat with him in his tent. There was a great hurry and scurry as Sarah and the servants set to work. They baked fresh bread and roasted a calf, and offered this to the visitors, with bowls of milk and cheese.

When the meal was finished, the men explained why they had come. Abraham and Sarah had grown old by this time, but God had good news for them. Very soon the son they longed for would be born. How surprised and pleased they were!

But what the men said next made them sad. God said that Sodom, the town where Lot now lived, was going to be destroyed.

The only good people in Sodom were Lot and his family. So God sent his messengers to warn Lot to escape before it was too late.

But Lot's family did not want to leave Sodom. Only
just in time, God's messengers hurried them all to
safety outside the town. They had not gone far before
there was a great rumbling. The ground trembled and
shook. Fire and ash rained down on Sodom and the
nearby towns and villages. The air was full of dust. But
still Lot's wife would not hurry. She stopped to look,
and was killed. Only Lot and his two daughters escaped.
God had saved their lives.

Isaac: the test

When God had called Abraham to leave Ur, he promised to make him the father of a great nation. He promised Abraham a son and so many descendants they would be as hard to count as the stars in the sky.

Through the long years of waiting, night after night, Abraham looked up at the stars and remembered God's promise. At last, when Abraham and Sarah were both old and had almost given up hope, Isaac was born. When Sarah looked at her baby son she was so happy that she laughed for joy.

The years passed and Isaac grew tall and strong. Then God decided to test Abraham.

'Abraham,' he said, 'I want you to take Isaac, your only son, whom you love so much, to the land of Moriah and offer him to me as a sacrifice.'

Abraham could hardly believe these cruel words.

Could God really want him to kill his son, after all God's promises? But Abraham had learnt always to trust God and obey him, so early next morning they set off. Isaac carried the wood, and Abraham had a knife, and hot cinders to start the fire.

They travelled for three days. Abraham could not bear to think of what he had to do when the journey was over. But he said nothing about it to Isaac. They were nearly at the place when Isaac said,

'Father, we have the wood and fire to offer God a sacrifice, but where is the lamb?'

Abraham swallowed hard. Then he said, 'God will provide the lamb.' But when they reached the place and the altar was built, and the wood piled on top, Abraham tied Isaac's hands and laid him on top. He raised the knife to kill his son . . .

But just at that moment God called out to him:

'Abraham! Stop! Don't touch the boy. I know now how much you trust me. I know you will obey, whatever I ask. Look in the bushes. You will find a ram caught by its horns. Sacrifice that.'

So Abraham freed his trembling son. Thankfully, joyfully, they killed the ram and roasted it on the altar. And God repeated all his wonderful promises of blessing, because when Abraham was put to the test he obeyed God.

A wife for Isaac

Sarah was dead; Abraham was now very old. It was time Isaac got married. But not to one of the local Canaanite women. Isaac must marry one of his own people.

Abraham's family lived far away, and he was too old to travel. So he called his trusted servant to him.

'I want you to go to Paddan-aram,' he said, 'where my brother Nahor lives, to choose a wife for Isaac.'

'But what if the girl refuses to come?' the man replied. 'Shall I take Isaac to her?'

'No, you must never do that,' said Abraham. 'For God has promised *this* land to my descendants.'

The servant took men and camels with him, and special presents for the girl and her family. The journey was long and weary but he arrived at last. He made his camels kneel down by the well, outside the town. It was late in the afternoon, and the women would soon be coming to fetch water. Which one was the right wife for Isaac?

The servant spoke to God, as he had heard his master do so often.

'Lord God,' he said, 'keep your promise to my master, Abraham. I need your help to find a wife for Isaac. I shall say to one of the girls, "Let me have a drink

from your water-jar." If she says, "I will bring water for your camels, too," let that be the right girl for Isaac.'

He had hardly finished praying when he saw a beautiful girl coming, with her water-jar on her shoulder. She filled her jar at the well and he asked for a drink. At once she gave him the water-jar, and when he had drunk as much as he wanted she brought water for all his camels.

This was the sign he had asked for, so the servant took a gold ring and two gold bracelets and gave them to the girl. Then he asked who she was, and whether he and his men could spend the night at her father's house.

'My name is Rebecca,' she said. 'I am Bethuel's daughter. My grandfather's name is Nahor.'

'Why, God has led me straight to my master's relatives,' the servant said, and thanked God for his help.

Rebecca left the man there and ran home to show off the presents and tell her family what had happened. When her brother Laban heard, he quickly went to greet the stranger and make him welcome.

Soon the camels were fed and the men had washed and were sitting down to a good hot meal. But Abraham's servant would not eat until he had told them why he had come. He spoke of Abraham and Isaac and

how God had blessed them. He told them how he had
prayed to God at the well, and how God had answered.
And he asked if they would allow Rebecca to go and be
Isaac's wife.

How could Bethuel and Laban refuse? It was clearly
God's plan. So the engagement presents were given,
and they enjoyed a celebration meal together.

Next morning, Abraham's servant was eager to go
home. And Rebecca agreed to set out at once, although
she was going with strangers, to a new home in a far-off
land.

And so, one evening, as he watched for their
return, Isaac saw camels coming. The men were eager
to tell their story. But Isaac was only half listening. He
was looking for the very first time at the beautiful girl
who had travelled so far to be his bride. The waiting
was over. Isaac took Rebecca to be his wife—and he
loved her.

The story of Jacob

Time passed, and twin sons—Esau and Jacob—were born to Isaac and Rebecca. When they were born, God said that they would become the fathers of two warring nations. Esau, the elder brother, would serve Jacob, the younger.

When Esau grew up he was a skilful hunter. He loved to be out on the hills. He hunted and killed wild animals which he brought home to make the tasty, spicy stews his father enjoyed so much. But Jacob was different. He was a quiet man. He spent his time at home. And he was Rebecca's favourite.

The lie

When Isaac was old he began to go blind. In those days, it was the custom for a father, before he died, to ask God's special blessing on the eldest son. Isaac decided it was time he gave Esau his blessing. But first he sent Esau out to hunt for meat to make a good stew.

Rebecca overheard what Isaac said to Esau, and she made up her mind that Jacob should have the blessing. Isaac was almost blind. Jacob could pretend to be Esau, and Isaac would never know.

So, while Esau was still out hunting, Rebecca made one of her tastiest, spiciest stews from the meat of two young goats. And she spread the goatskins over Jacob's smooth arms and neck to make them feel like Esau's rough, hairy skin.

Jacob dressed up in his brother's clothes, and took the meal in to his father. The lovely smell from the food, and the feel of the skins, deceived Isaac. But he thought the voice sounded different.

'Are you really Esau?' he asked.

'I am,' Jacob lied.

So Isaac prayed that God would give his richest blessing, the blessing of the first son, to Jacob.

When Esau himself arrived, the truth came out. But it was too late. The blessing had been given. Esau was so angry with Jacob that Rebecca was afraid he would kill him. So she persuaded Isaac to let Jacob go to her people in Paddan-aram, to find a wife.

The dream

Jacob journeyed north, alone and afraid. At sunset he reached a wild and stony valley. Here he lay down to sleep, using a stone for his pillow. As he slept, he dreamed he saw a great staircase stretching up to heaven, with angels going up and down it. At the top stood God himself, and he was speaking to Jacob.

'I will give the land on which you lie to you and your descendants,' God said. 'I am with you. I will look after you wherever you go, and I will bring you back to this land.'

When Jacob woke up, he was very afraid, despite the comforting words. He was certain that it was God's voice he had heard. Jacob made God a promise.

'If you will be with me and protect me,' he said, 'and bring me home safely, then you will be my God.'

Jacob meets his match

Jacob reached his mother's homeland at last. He had
stopped beside a well to ask about his uncle Laban. A
girl came out to water her flocks—and it was his cousin
Rachel, Laban's daughter! Jacob wept for joy as he told
her who he was.

Laban welcomed him as one of the family. A month
went by, with Jacob working for Laban. Then Laban
asked Jacob how much pay he wanted.

'I will work for you for seven years if you will let
me marry your daughter Rachel,' Jacob said.

Laban agreed; and Jacob loved Rachel so much that
the seven years passed like seven days. But when the
wedding-day came, Laban cheated and gave Jacob his
elder daughter, Leah. He made the excuse that in his
country the elder daughter must marry before the
younger one. Laban was quite happy to let Jacob marry
Rachel as well. But Jacob had to work for his uncle
without pay for another seven years.

So Jacob had two wives—and an unhappy home.

Jacob loved Rachel more than Leah, which made
Leah unhappy. But Leah had children. And Rachel,
although she longed for children, had none. As the

years went by, Leah had six sons and a daughter. Then, at last, Rachel had her first son. She called him Joseph.

The journey home

By this time Jacob was longing to go back home. But he had helped his uncle to become rich, and Laban did not want to let him go.

'Stay with me, and I will pay you whatever you like,' he said. This was Jacob's chance.

Jacob agreed. 'And for wages I will take the black sheep and goats, and the ones that are speckled or spotted,' he said. Laban tried to cheat him, but God helped Jacob, and his flocks increased. Jacob became rich, but Laban's sons began to hate him.

He knew that Laban would never let him go, so he waited until his uncle was busy shearing the sheep. Then he fled across the River Euphrates with his wives and children, his servants, and his flocks. Laban followed, but he could not persuade Jacob to return.

Jacob continued on his way home to Canaan. As they got nearer, he felt more and more afraid. Was Esau still angry with him? He sent messengers ahead to make his peace with Esau. But they returned, saying that Esau was on his way with 400 men. Jacob turned to God for help.

'O God,' he prayed, 'you told me to return. I don't deserve any of your goodness to me. Save me now from Esau's anger.'

He chose a great number of sheep and goats, camels and cattle and asses, to give as a present to Esau. And he sent his servants on ahead with them. Then he and his wives and children crossed the River Jabbok at the ford.

That night, when Jacob was alone with his fears, a strange thing happened. A man came and wrestled with him all night till daybreak. Jacob did not know him, but he knew he came from God. And he would not let him go until he had God's blessing.

After that night Jacob always walked with a limp, but he was a changed man with a new name—no longer Jacob, the man who had cheated his brother, but Israel, the man who had come face to face with God.

As the sun rose, Jacob saw Esau and his men coming towards him. He had expected trouble, but instead Esau ran to meet him, and hugged him. Old quarrels were forgotten in the joy of meeting again.

'Who are these?' said Esau, as the family gathered round. 'And what were the flocks I met?'

'The flocks are a present,' said Jacob. 'Please take them. For when I saw the look of loving welcome on your face, it was like looking into the face of God himself.'

Joseph and his brothers

Jacob had twelve sons: Reuben, Simeon, Levi, Judah, Issachar and Zebulun (sons of Leah); Gad and Asher (sons of Zilpah, Leah's servant-girl); Dan and Naphtali (sons of Bilhah, Rachel's servant-girl); and Joseph and Benjamin (Rachel's sons).

Joseph was Jacob's favourite. He should have known it would lead to trouble. But Rachel had died when Benjamin was born, and Jacob had loved Rachel so much. He could not help loving her sons more than the other children. And he did not even try to be fair. He spoilt Joseph, and dressed him in a special coat, one that should have been given to Jacob's first son, Reuben.

This made all the brothers jealous, and they hated

Joseph. There was more trouble because Joseph had dreams—and in his dreams his brothers and his father, too, were all bowing down to him. Even Jacob was cross when Joseph boasted about his dreams.

One day, Jacob sent Joseph out to check that his

brothers and the flocks were well. But when they saw Joseph coming, they decided to kill him. Reuben, who was hoping to rescue the boy later, persuaded them not to kill him there and then.

Sold as a slave

'Throw him into this dry well,' he said—and they agreed. But while Reuben was away looking after the sheep, some traders passed by on their way to Egypt. The other brothers sold Joseph to them for twenty pieces of silver. When Reuben returned it was too late.

They took Joseph's special coat and stained it with

blood. Then they went home and showed it to their father. Jacob wept bitter tears, thinking that wild animals had torn Joseph to pieces. He would not be comforted.

Meanwhile, Joseph had been sold as a slave to Potiphar, an officer of the king of Egypt. Joseph was a slave in a foreign land, but he was not alone. God was with him. And Potiphar was soon so pleased with his new slave that he put him in charge of his household and all his business.

Joseph was good-looking, and Potiphar's wife fell in love with him. But he was loyal to his master and would not make love to her. Then Potiphar's wife grew angry and told lies about Joseph to her husband. She said that Joseph had attacked her.

In the king's prison

Potiphar was furious. He had Joseph flung into the king's prison. But God was still with him. He won the prison governor's trust and was put in charge of all the other prisoners. One of them was the king of Egypt's butler—the man who served his wine. Another was the king's baker.

One night both men had strange dreams. Next morning, when Joseph came to bring their food, he found them very worried. What could these dreams mean? In Egypt, in those days, people took their dreams seriously. Every dream had a meaning.

'God can show us the meaning of dreams,' Joseph said. So the butler and the baker told Joseph their dreams and God showed Joseph what they meant.

The butler had dreamt of a vine with three branches. He picked the grapes, and squeezed the juice into the king's cup and gave it to him.

'In three days' time,' Joseph said, 'the king will set you free and you will have your old job back. Please be kind enough to mention me to the king and help me to get out of prison.'

The butler promised.

The baker had dreamt he was carrying three bread-baskets on his head, full of pastries for the king. But the birds were eating them.

'In three days' time,' Joseph said, 'the king will bring you out of prison. But he will cut off your head.'

Everything happened just as Joseph had said. But the butler forgot all about his promise.

The king's dream

Two years later, the king had a strange dream, and no one could explain it. Then the butler remembered Joseph, and he was brought out of prison. The king told him his dream.

The king was standing by the River Nile, when seven fat cows came out of the river. Then came seven thin cows—and the thin cows ate up the fat ones!

God showed Joseph what the dream meant.

'There will be seven years of good harvests, followed by seven hungry years,' Joseph told the king. 'If you are wise, you will store food in the good years so that your people do not starve in the bad ones.'

The king was delighted to have his dream explained. Joseph was clearly a man of God. There could be no better man to arrange for the grain and crops to be stored. So the king put his own ring on Joseph's finger, and a gold chain round his neck, and made him second-in-command over the whole land of Egypt.

After seven years, as Joseph had said, the crops did not grow, and in many lands there was little to eat. But in Egypt Joseph opened up the store-houses and sold food to the people.

In Canaan his father and brothers were already short of grain to make bread. At last Jacob decided to send his sons—all of them except Benjamin—to Egypt.

As Jacob's ten sons stood before the governor, asking if they might buy grain, none of them recognized their long-lost brother! But Joseph knew at once who they were. He decided to see if they were still as cruel as they had been. So he looked at them sternly.

'You are spies!' he said—and flung them into prison. He set them free after three days. But he made them promise to bring Benjamin with them next time. And he kept Simeon as a hostage, to make sure that they did. Then he ordered his servants to put the money his brothers had paid for the grain back in their sacks.

When the brothers opened their sacks and found the money, they were very worried.

Sadly they travelled back to Canaan with the grain. Next time they must take Benjamin. But how could they persuade Jacob to part with his youngest son? When the food was finished there was no choice. Benjamin had to go with them or they would starve.

Again they stood before the governor of Egypt— and when Joseph saw Benjamin he could hardly hold back his tears. The brothers knelt before Joseph.

'How is the old man, your father?' he said. 'And is

this your youngest brother?'

Then Joseph's servants prepared a meal and the brothers sat down to eat. When the food was brought, Benjamin was given five times as much as the others. But still Joseph did not tell them who he was.

Next morning, when the sacks were filled with grain, Joseph told his servants to hide his own silver cup in Benjamin's sack.

The brothers had not gone far when Joseph's men caught up with them. They were looking for the 'thief' who had stolen Joseph's cup. When Benjamin's sack was opened, there, to the brothers' horror, lay the missing cup. They all returned to the city, and fell at Joseph's feet.

'The man in whose sack the cup was found shall be my slave,' said Joseph, testing them. 'The rest of you are free to go.'

But the brothers would not hear of it. They could not bear to tell their father that this son, too, had been taken from him.

Judah spoke. 'If Benjamin does not return with us our father will die of grief. I promised to bring the boy back safely. Let me be your slave in his place.'

When Joseph heard this, he knew his brothers were truly sorry for what they had done to him all those years before. He sent his servants out of the room— and then burst into tears.

'I am Joseph,' he said. 'Is my father still alive?' There was dismay on all their faces. Now Joseph could really pay them back. What would he do to them?

But Joseph was speaking again. 'Don't be afraid. It was God who sent me here in order to save all our lives. The harvest will be bad for five more years and many will starve to death. Go home and bring the rest of the family here, to live near me in the land of Goshen.' And he hugged them all, as the tears ran down his face.

So Jacob and Joseph's brothers, their wives and children, their servants and cattle and flocks, left Canaan and came to Egypt. Joseph took Jacob to the palace to meet the king. And then they all settled in Goshen, the best part of the land.

Moses hears God's call

Time passed, and Jacob's descendants—the Israelites—
grew into a strong and powerful nation. The Egyptians
began to be afraid of them. A new king came to the
throne and he decided to act before it was too late.

He made the Israelites his slaves. Cruel slave-drivers
forced them to make bricks to build new cities for the
king. They were kept hard at work from dawn to
dark—but still their numbers grew.

So the king gave orders that every Israelite baby boy
should be drowned in the River Nile.

About this time an Israelite woman called Jochebed
had a baby. She already had two children, a boy called
Aaron, and a girl called Miriam. When she saw that the
new baby was a boy she was terribly afraid. She hid him
in the house for three months; but babies won't stay
quiet and still for long. What was she to do?

Then she had an idea. She made a basket out of reeds and covered it with tar, to make it watertight. She put the baby inside. Then she took the basket and placed it among the tall reeds at the river's edge. She told Miriam to keep watch.

Very soon, the king's daughter came down to the

river to bathe, as Jochebed knew she would. And when she saw the basket she sent her servant to fetch it. They opened the lid, and there inside was the loveliest baby she had ever seen. And he was crying! The princess knew that this was an Israelite baby. But she had no children and she decided to bring him up as her own son. She would call him Moses.

The princess turned and there, right beside her, was Miriam, offering to fetch a nurse for the baby. And of course the nurse Miriam ran to find was the baby's own mother!

So Moses grew up in the king's palace, learning all that the Egyptians could teach him. But he never forgot that he was an Israelite. And it made him sad to see how cruel the Egyptian slave-drivers were to his people.

One day he saw an Egyptian lashing one of the Israelites with a whip. Moses sprang at the man and killed him. Now his own life was in danger, for the king would hear what he had done. So Moses left Egypt and fled to the safety of the desert.

He was there a long time, working as a shepherd in the land of Midian. In Egypt the troubles of the Israelites grew worse.

One day, as Moses was out minding his father-in-law's flocks, he saw a very strange sight. There was a bush which seemed to be on fire. But the fire did not burn it up.

Moses went to have a closer look.

'Stand back,' said a voice. 'And take off your shoes—you are on holy ground.'

Moses was very afraid. The voice came again:

'I am God—the God your fathers knew and worshipped. I have seen the cruel sufferings of my people the Israelites. You are to go to the king of Egypt and set my people free. Bring them here to me.'

'But what am I to say? What am I to do? They won't listen to me,' said Moses. 'Please send someone else!'

'No,' said God. 'I have chosen you. Take your brother Aaron with you to do the speaking, and I will give you the words—and power to work wonders. Am I not the living God?'

Pharaoh says no

Moses and Aaron stood before Pharaoh, king of Egypt.

'We have a request to make,' they said. 'The Lord God of Israel says, "Let my people go out into the desert for a festival." '

'I don't know your God,' answered the king. 'What is he to me? I will not let the Israelites go.'

The king was angry.

'From now on no one is to give the Israelites the straw they need to mix with the clay to make their bricks,' he said. 'Let them find their own. And they must make just as many bricks as before.'

This was terrible. In despair, Moses cried out to God for help.

'You will see what I shall do to the king of Egypt,'
God said. 'I am God. I shall make Pharaoh let my
people go. I shall set them free and you will lead them
out of Egypt. Go to the king again. Tell him I shall
bring terrible trouble on Egypt if he will not do as I ask.
Then all Egypt will know that I really am God.'

Moses and Aaron stood before the king again.

'Show me a miracle, if you really come from God,'
he said.

So Aaron threw down the strong stick he
carried—and it became a snake. But the Egyptian
magicians did the same, so the king sent Moses and
Aaron away.

Then God took action, as he had warned. Terrible
things began to happen. Every time, God sent a
warning to the king beforehand. But the king did not
believe him. He would not listen.

First the water in the River Nile turned blood-red. It
smelt dreadful, and all the fish died.

A week later the whole land was swarming with
frogs. The king begged Moses to take them away—but
still he would not let the people go.

Next came swarms of insects and flies. They were
everywhere, except in Goshen where the Israelites
lived.

'You can go!' cried Pharaoh—but then he changed
his mind.

Then the cattle began to die—everywhere, except in
Goshen. But the king still said no.

Everyone had painful boils, even the magicians. But
the king still said no.

Moses and Aaron stood before him yet again.

'God says, "You have seen my power. There is
more trouble to come if you do not let the Israelites go.
Tomorrow there will be hail"!'

No one had ever seen hail like it. It flattened the crops and killed the cattle out in the fields. The hail fell everywhere—except in Goshen.

Next came swarms of locusts, which ate up every green thing. And after that, pitch-darkness for three days. But the king still tried to bargain with God. He would not let the people go.

Then the most terrible thing of all happened. In a single night the eldest son of every family in Egypt died—from the king's son and heir to the son of his lowest slave.

But in Goshen the Israelites were safe. God had told them what to do.

Every Israelite family killed a lamb that night, and splashed some of the blood on the doorposts of the house. They roasted the lamb and ate it with herbs and flat loaves of bread, made quickly without yeast. And death 'passed over' their houses. (That is why for ever after, once a year, the people of Israel ate this special 'Passover' meal, and remembered how God had saved them.)

Next day the Egyptians could not wait to get rid of the Israelites. They even gave them gold and silver jewelry and fine clothes to take with them.

But still the king tried to stop them. As soon as they had gone he called out the army. The soldiers leapt into their swift, light chariots and raced after the Israelites.

By the time the Israelites reached the lakes and marshes near the border, the Egyptian army was close behind. There was water in front of them, and soldiers behind them. The people were terrified.

But Moses stretched out his arm, and God sent an east wind. All night it blew, clearing a pathway through the water for the Israelites to cross in safety.

But when the Egyptians tried to follow, the water rushed back and the king's whole army was drowned. So God saved his people and led them out of Egypt to freedom.

'Manna' in the desert

The people of Israel had escaped from Egypt. They were no longer slaves. They were free! Moses and Aaron's sister, Miriam, took her tambourine and led the women as they danced and sang for joy.

'Sing to the Lord, because he has won a glorious victory; he has thrown the horses and their riders into the sea.'

But before long they forgot their cruel slavery in Egypt. They forgot about the slave-drivers with their savage whips. All they could think of was the food they had enjoyed in Egypt. The fish! Those juicy melons! And the leeks and onions and cucumbers! What was there to eat in the desert?

So they began to grumble. They turned against Moses and Aaron.

'It would have been better to die in Egypt,' they said, 'than to starve to death in this desert.'

God heard the grumbles, and he spoke to Moses.

'Tell the people I will give them all they need. I have saved their lives. I will give them food. There will be meat tonight, and a new kind of bread tomorrow—every morning from now on. Except on Fridays, when I will give you enough for two days so that no one has to work on Saturday, my Sabbath day of rest '

Moses told the people what God had said and, sure enough, that evening at dusk a great flock of birds called quails settled to rest around the tents! So the people had their meat.

Next morning, when the sun dried the dew, there on the ground all around the camp was the special bread God had promised. It lay there like frost, and the people gathered it quickly before the hot sun melted it. They called it 'manna'. It tasted very good—like biscuits made with honey.

All the time they were in the desert God gave the people manna to eat—day by day. They never had to go hungry.

But there were other troubles. The hot sun burned down, and there was very little water in the desert. So the people began to grumble again.

'Give us water, Moses. Did you bring us here to die of thirst?'

Again Moses cried to God for help.

'Take your strong stick and strike the rock with it,' God said. 'You will have enough water for everyone to drink as much as they want.'

And again God did just as he had said. Water poured from the rock. The people were wrong to put God to the test, but he did not fail them.

For forty years God looked after his people in the desert. He kept every one of his promises to them. Day by day he fed them and gave them water, to teach them to depend on him and to trust him.

The ten laws of God

Moses led the people of Israel from the borders of Egypt, through the desert to Mount Sinai, where God had told him to bring them. God himself went ahead of them, to show them the way. The people knew he was there, because out in front all day was a column of cloud, and at night a column of fire. When they reached Sinai they set up camp at the foot of the mountain.

God spoke to the people through Moses.

'I have brought you safely out of Egypt. I want you to be my own special people. Will you obey me?'

With one voice the people answered, 'Yes!'

Then they set to work, washing their clothes and cleaning the camp to get ready for a meeting with God.

'The day after tomorrow,' God said, 'I will come down on Mount Sinai where everyone can see me.'

On the third morning there was thunder and lightning and thick cloud on the mountain. The people trembled. They knew that God was near.

Moses and Aaron went up into the mountain alone, and God gave them the ten great laws his people must keep.

'I am God,' he said. 'You are to honour and serve me, and me alone.

'Do not make idols, or bow down to them.

'Treat my name with respect.

'Keep my day of rest, the seventh day.

'Show respect to your father and mother.

'Do not kill another human being.

'Husbands and wives—be loyal to one another, don't go off with another woman or another man.

'Do not steal.

'Do not tell lies.

'Do not be greedy for the things that other people have.'

These are the ten commandments of God.

God explained to Moses how these laws applied in all sorts of different situations. And Moses explained to the people.

The people all agreed to obey God's laws.

God said he would write them on stone tablets for the people to keep. And Moses went up into the mountain to receive them.

But this time he was away so long that the people grew angry and impatient.

'We don't know what has happened to Moses, who led us out of Egypt,' they said to Aaron. 'So make us a new god to lead us.'

Aaron asked the people to give him their gold earrings. Then he melted them down and made a gold bull, like one of the gods of Egypt. He built an altar and held a feast. And the people said,

'This is our god that brought us out of Egypt.'

And they made a great noise, singing and dancing.

When God saw how quickly his people had broken their word and turned to other gods, he was angry. And when Moses went down the mountain and saw what the people were doing, he was angry, too.

He threw down the stone tablets of the law and they broke in pieces. And he ground the gold bull to powder.

'You have done a terrible thing,' he said.

But Moses still loved the people. And he asked God to forgive them and let them have a second chance. So God wrote out his laws again.

This time, when Moses returned, there was no gold bull and no feasting. The people listened to Moses as he taught them the law of God. The agreement, the 'covenant', was sealed at last between God and his people.

God's special tent

God gave Moses a great many laws for his people at Sinai—laws about right and wrong; laws for health; laws about punishment. He told his people how to behave, how to treat one another—and how to honour and serve him.

God is good. He takes a delight in all that is right and just and true. He hates to see evil and wrong. In those days there was a great deal wrong with the religion of the nations who lived in the lands close to the Israelites. They worshipped many gods. Their feasts were an excuse to get drunk for days. They treated their women badly. They practised magic. They even killed their own children and offered them up to idols. God hated all these things.

'Those nations have disgusted me with all their evil practices,' he said. 'You must not follow their customs. You are to be holy, to belong only to me.'

So God told Moses the kind of feasts and sacrifices and worship he wanted—and Moses explained to the people.

'I have promised to be with you always,' God said. 'So build me a special tent (the tabernacle) like one of your own. Make it of goatskin, and line it with fine linen—scarlet, purple and blue, and embroidered with figures of winged beasts. Make a courtyard round the tent, for the sacrifices; and divide the inside of the tent with curtains to make two rooms.

'No one but the priests may enter the first room. I want you to make a golden altar, a table and a lampstand holding seven lamps for this part of my tent.

'The inner room is to be set apart for me. Just once a year, on the Day of Atonement, the high priest may come in to make peace for the sins of the people.

'I want you to make a box of acacia-wood (the ark of the covenant) covered with gold for my special room, to hold the tablets on which my laws are written. Make a lid of pure gold, and two beasts of gold with wings outspread to cover it. This is where I will meet with you.'

The people did all that God said. They gladly gave their gold and jewels, silver and bronze, linen and animal-skins for the tent of God. They brought oil for the lamps and spices to burn as incense, scenting the air. And their best craftsmen set to work—spinning and weaving and dyeing; smoothing and polishing and engraving precious stones; beating and shaping the gold and silver. So God's tent was made to his design, and it was very beautiful.

When it was finished a cloud covered the tent, and the glory of God filled it. This was God's sign that he had come to be with his people.

God chose Aaron as the first high priest, to be in charge of all the feasts and sacrifices. His sons served as priests, and the Levites (the family descended from Jacob's son, Levi) helped them.

Moses explained to the people that although God was with them and wanted them to come to him as friends, they could not come just as they were. God is absolutely good. Nothing—no one—that is wrong or spoiled by sin can live in his presence. Every single human being falls short of God's perfect goodness. Sin builds a barrier between man and God. The penalty for sin—for breaking God's law—is death.

But because God loved his people, he accepted the death of a lamb or a kid instead of the death of the man or woman who had done wrong. So he made it possible for his people to pay the penalty of sin and come to him as his friends.

Aaron and the priests and the Levites were put in charge of the sacrifices—the sin offerings, the guilt offerings and the peace offerings. Once a year, on the Day of Atonement, Aaron offered up special sacrifices for the sins of the whole nation, to put himself and the people right with God.

God also commanded his people to keep each Saturday (the seventh day of the week) as a day of rest, the 'Sabbath'. God made the world in six days, and rested on the seventh. His people must stop work too, and keep the seventh day of the week as a day for rest and for remembering God's goodness.*

*The Jews still keep Saturday as the 'Sabbath'. But because Jesus rose from death on a Sunday, Christians keep that day of the week as their special day.

God gave them feasts, too—feasts for special events and special times of year. In spring there was the Passover and Feast of Unleavened Bread, when they remembered the escape from Egypt. In early summer was the Feast of the Firstfruits of Harvest. In the autumn they enjoyed Harvest Festival, the Feast of Trumpets and the Feast of Tents.

These are the things God told his people to do. This was the kind of worship he wanted. As they looked at his special tent they knew God was near. On the 'Sabbath' they rested and remembered that God made the world and everything in it. On feast days they enjoyed a special meal and rejoiced together at all God's goodness to them. And the sacrifices reminded them all the time of their own sin and God's perfect goodness— but also of his love which made it possible for his people to come to him and be his friends.

Rebellion!

From Mount Sinai, where God gave them his laws, the Israelites moved north through the desert to the borders of Canaan—the land God had promised to give them.

At Kadesh they chose one man from each of the twelve tribes (the descendants of Jacob's twelve sons), and sent them to spy out the land. It was the time of year when the first grapes are ripe.

After forty days the men returned—two of them carrying a huge cluster of grapes.

'Canaan is a good land,' they said. 'Just look at the grapes and figs and pomegranates we have brought back with us! But the cities are strong—and there are men as big as giants. If we go in they will crush us like grasshoppers.'

The people were in despair when they heard this.

'Why did we leave Egypt?' they cried. 'We must go back.'

But Joshua and Caleb, two of the spies, spoke up.

'Don't let the others frighten you,' they said. 'Canaan is a good land—and you are forgetting God. If he goes with us, we have nothing to fear. He will give us the land. Don't turn against him now.'

But the people refused to listen.

Then God said to them,

'When will you learn to trust me? How quickly you forget all that I have done for you. Now, because you have refused to trust me, you will wander in the desert for forty years—until everyone who saw my wonders in Egypt is dead. All except Joshua and Caleb. They will live to go in and possess the land, because they trusted in me.'

The people were sad at heart when they heard this. Yet some still refused to take God at his word. They went out to fight the Canaanites, against God's orders. And they were beaten!

Time passed, and the people grew weary of life in the desert. They grumbled about their leaders and turned against them. There was open rebellion in the camp.

'What right have Moses and Aaron to lord it over us?' they said.

Then Moses answered,

'Let God decide who is to lead his people. Every

tribe must choose a leader and write his name on an almond-branch. Aaron will be the leader for his own tribe—the Levites. Tonight we will put the twelve almond-branches in God's tent. The man whose branch comes into flower will be God's chosen leader.'

They did as Moses said. And next morning there were buds and flowers—and ripe almonds too!—on Aaron's branch. But the others were bare. So the rebels had to be quiet.

After some years, Aaron died—and the grumbling began again.

'Why did we leave Egypt? There is no food or water here. We are tired of eating manna day after day.'

This time God punished the rebels. Poisonous snakes came into the camp, and many people died. Then the rest came to their senses.

'Moses,' they said, 'it was very wrong of us to speak against God. Ask him to take the snakes away.'

So Moses prayed, and God said:

'Make a bronze snake and fasten it to a pole for everyone to see. Those who are bitten need only look at the bronze snake—and they will live.' So everyone who believed God and did as he said was made well again.

Rahab and the spies

Forty years passed. Moses died—and God chose Joshua to take his place as leader. The time had come to conquer Canaan—the promised land. The Israelites camped on the far side of the River Jordan, opposite the city of Jericho. Joshua sent two spies across the river.

To avoid suspicion, they stayed the night at the house of Rahab, a prostitute. But the king of Jericho got to know of it, and sent his men to capture them. Rahab quickly hid the spies on the roof of her house, under the flax she had spread out to dry. When the king's men came, she told them that the two strangers had gone.

Then she went to the spies and said:
'I know that God has given this land to the

Israelites. We have heard how he brought you out of Egypt, and we are all afraid. Promise me that my family and I will be safe when you take the city.'

'You have saved our lives,' said the men. 'We promise, if you don't tell anyone what we've been doing.'

Rahab lived in a house built into the city wall. So she let the men down from the window by a rope. And they escaped to report back to Joshua. But before they left, they gave her a red cord to tie to the window, so that they would know which house was hers when they captured the city.

The fortress-city of Jericho

It was spring. The snows had melted on the mountains in the north, and the River Jordan overflowed its banks. The people of Israel prepared to cross the river. There was no bridge, and no ford—but God had told them this was the day when they must go across. The priests were in front, with the special box that held God's laws. And the people watched to see what would happen.

As they stepped into the river there was a distant roar—and the water-level fell. Upstream, the river banks collapsed, damming the whole stream. The water began to pile up. But near Jericho the Israelites were able to walk across the river-bed. God, who had brought them out of Egypt, had shown his power again—to bring them into the promised land.

When the people were safely across, they carried twelve stones from the river-bed—one for each of the tribes. And they heaped them up on the bank.

'Let these stones be a sign,' God said. 'And when your children see them in years to come, you can tell them the wonderful way I brought you into this land.'

Then the water broke through the dam and filled the river again till it overflowed its banks, just as before. Only the heap of stones remained to show what had happened.

The Israelites set up camp near Jericho. It was time for the Feast of Passover. The following day they made bread and, for the first time, roasted corn grown in Canaan, the promised land. From that day on, there was no more 'manna'. For their time in the desert was over. Now they could enjoy all the fruits of the land.

Jericho was a city with a long history. It was surrounded by high walls many feet thick. Now the town gates were shut and barred. No one could get in or out because of the Israelites.

God spoke to Joshua:

'Jericho is yours. I will give you the city, its king and all its great men. This is what you must do.

'Every day for six days you must march once round the city. Seven priests must walk in front of the men who are carrying my special box, sounding their trumpets. The rest must march in silence.

'On the seventh day, you are to walk round the city seven times. And when the trumpets sound, let the people give a great shout. The city walls will collapse, and Jericho will be yours.'

Joshua gave the people their orders, and they did exactly as God had told them. On the seventh day, they marched round seven times, the trumpets sounded, and Joshua said to the people:

'Shout!—for God has given us the city.'

So they gave a great shout, and the walls crashed down. Then they went in and took the city. No one was safe, except Rahab and her family—as the spies had promised. They took silver and gold, bronze and iron to add to the treasures of God's special tent. Then they set fire to the city. So God gave his people their first great victory in Canaan. And Joshua's fame spread far and wide, so that all the nations feared him.

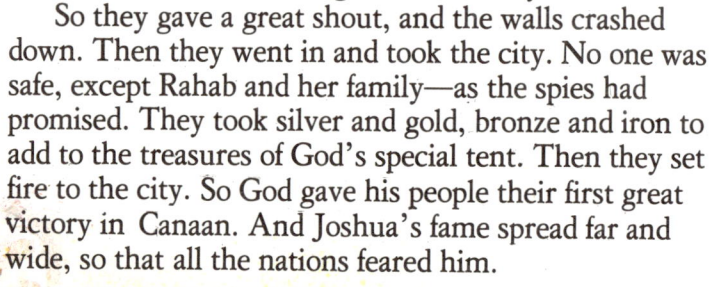

Israel in the promised land

God had told his people to destroy Jericho. They were to take nothing for themselves. But one man—Achan—disobeyed. He stole a beautiful cloak and some gold and silver.

No one saw him. But God knew. And when the men of Israel marched against the fortress at Ai, they were beaten. God would not go with them and give them victory unless they obeyed him.

Achan was punished. And Joshua got ready to attack Ai again. This time God told him to take the city by surprise.

Joshua made a clever plan. That night he sent some of his best men into hiding on the far side of the city. Next morning he led the army towards the city gates. When the men of Ai came out to fight, Joshua ordered his men to turn and run, drawing the enemy soldiers away from the city.

Then Joshua signalled to the men who were in hiding. They marched straight into the city and set it on fire. When Joshua and his men saw the smoke, they turned. And the soldiers from Ai were caught between the two Israelite forces.

The people who lived at the nearby town of Gibeon, heard how Joshua had destroyed Jericho and defeated the men of Ai. They did not want to die. How could they persuade Joshua to make peace?

Some days later, Joshua saw a group of tired travellers coming towards his camp. Their sandals were worn through and their clothes were ragged.

'Who are you?' Joshua asked. 'And where do you come from?'

'We have come from a far-off land,' they said.

'We heard how God brought you out of Egypt. And we have come to make peace. See how mouldy our bread is? It was freshly baked when we started out. And our clothes are worn out with the journey.'

Joshua and his people made a treaty of friendship with the men, and promised to keep it.

Three days later, they discovered that the 'weary travellers' had come from nearby Gibeon! They were very angry. But they kept their word.

Meanwhile the kings of the small city-states in Canaan joined forces to meet the enemy.

Joshua led his men in two fierce campaigns, one in the south, one in the north. They won great battles. Little by little the Israelites conquered the land of Canaan, the 'promised land'. But they did not manage to drive out all the enemy nations.

Caleb had gone with Joshua and the ten other men to spy out the land for Moses, long before. Now he was an old man of eighty-five. But he was as strong and brave as ever. And he trusted God.

'Give me the hill-country where those giant men live,' he said to Joshua. 'With God's help, I shall drive them out.'

So Joshua gave him the town of Hebron. And Caleb drove the giants out!

Joshua divided up the land of Canaan. Each tribe had its own territory. The Israelites began to settle in and farm the land.

When Joshua was very old, he called all the people together.

'God has given us all the good things he promised,' Joshua said. 'Every promise he made has been kept. Now will you promise to keep the agreement with him? Will you serve him?'

'We will serve the Lord. He is our God,' the people answered. And as long as Joshua lived they kept their promise.

Gideon's three hundred

The years passed. Joshua died—and soon the people forgot all that God had done for them. They forgot their promise to serve only God. They began to worship the gods of the nations around them.

Then from north and south, east and west, their enemies began to make trouble. Each time the Israelites came to their senses and cried to God for help, he sent a champion to drive the enemy back:

Othniel,
Ehud,
Shamgar,
Deborah and Barak,
Gideon . . .

The trouble in Gideon's day came from a tribe of desert raiders—the Midianites. They rode in on their camels, too many to count, like an army of locusts. They seized the Israelites' sheep and cattle and donkeys. They ate up all the crops.

The people of Israel cried out to God for help.

And God sent his messenger to Gideon.

God says, 'I am sending you to rescue Israel from the Midianites.'

Gideon gasped.

He took a lot of convincing.

He asked for proof.

'I am going to put some wool on the ground,' he said. 'Tomorrow morning, if there is dew on the wool but not on the ground, I'll know you are going to use me to rescue Israel.'

Next morning he was able to wring a bowlful of

Samson the strong

Even though God rescued his people so often, they soon forgot him. They worshipped the gods of the nations all around—gods of weather and gods of war. And before long they were in trouble again.

Most often of all, trouble came from the Philistines, in the south-west. For forty years they ruled over the Israelites.

Then one day God sent a message to a man called Manoah and his wife, who lived in Zorah.

'You will have a son,' God said, 'who will grow up to deliver Israel from the Philistines.'

Now Manoah and his wife had been married for years and had no children. So they were amazed at this news. But in due course, to their joy, the boy was born. They called him Samson. And they never cut his hair. It was a sign that Samson belonged to God in a special way. So Samson grew up and he was very strong.

One day, as Samson was walking through the vineyards, a lion sprang out at him. Samson strangled the lion with his bare hands. Then he knew that God had given him special strength—and he began to use

that strength against the Philistines. Soon everyone was talking about him.

'Have you heard how Samson set the Philistine cornfields ablaze? He tied lighted torches to the tails of a pack of jackals and they burnt the whole crop.'

'Have you heard how Samson killed a thousand Philistines—with no weapon but a donkey's jawbone?'

'Have you heard how he escaped from Gaza? He lifted the gate and gateposts clean out of the ground.'

'Have you heard . . . ?'

The Philistines ground their teeth in fury. They were out for Samson's blood!

Samson fell in love with a beautiful Philistine girl called Delilah—and that gave his enemies their chance.

'If you love me, tell me the secret of your strength,' she pleaded, day after day. (The Philistine kings had promised her 1100 silver coins if she got the right answer.)

At first Samson teased her.

'Tie me up with seven new bowstrings and I'll be as weak as anyone else.'

'Weave my long hair into your loom . . .'

But in the end she wore him down and he told her the truth.

'My hair has never been cut,' he said. 'It is a sign that I belong to God. My strength comes from him.'

Delilah stroked his head until he fell asleep. Then she betrayed him to his enemies. The Philistines came in and shaved off his hair—and Samson's strength was gone. They blinded him and brought him in chains to their city of Gaza. There he was forced to grind corn at the prison mill.

Time passed. Samson's hair grew long again. He really knew now that his strength was not his own. God had given it to him for a special purpose.

The Philistines held a feast in honour of their god, Dagon. They brought Samson into Dagon's temple to make fun of him. The place was crowded with people. Samson prayed to God for strength as he grasped the two central pillars and pulled with all his might.

The building crashed down, killing all who were in it. It was Samson's last act and his greatest.

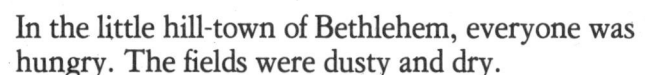

Ruth leaves home

In the little hill-town of Bethlehem, everyone was hungry. The fields were dusty and dry.

'We have no food left,' Elimelech said one day to Naomi, his wife. 'Pack everything we need. Tomorrow we must take the boys on a long journey.'

'Where are we going?' Naomi asked.

'Across the River Jordan to Moab,' Elimelech replied. 'They have plenty to eat there.'

So Elimelech and Naomi, with their two sons, went to live in the country of Moab.

The boys grew up and married two Moabite girls, Orpah and Ruth. Elimelech died. About ten years later, both Naomi's sons died, too. And she was left all alone.

Then news came from Bethlehem that the long famine was over. Naomi decided to go back home.

'You can't make that journey all by yourself,' said Ruth, and Orpah agreed with her. So Orpah and Ruth left their own homes and set out for Bethlehem with Naomi. But on the way, Naomi tried to persuade them to go back, and marry again. They did not want to leave her, but she insisted.

Orpah cried as Naomi kissed her goodbye—but she went back home. Ruth refused to go.

'Don't ask me to leave you,' she said. 'I will go wherever you go. Your people will be my people, and your God will be my God.'

So the two women went on their way together.

It was April when they arrived in Bethlehem. The farmers were beginning to harvest the barley. Naomi's old friends were very excited to see her again. But Naomi was sad. She was home, at last, but her husband and sons were dead.

Naomi and Ruth were very poor. Each day, Ruth went out into the fields. She walked behind the reapers, picking up the corn they left. In the evening she ground it to make flour for bread. Although she did not know it, the field she had chosen to work in belonged to a rich relative of Naomi. His name was Boaz.

'Who is that?' Boaz asked one day, when he noticed Ruth.

'The foreign girl, who came here with Naomi,' his workmen answered. 'She has been hard at work since early morning.'

'Stay in this field with my workers,' Boaz said to Ruth. 'And when you are thirsty, drink from the water-jars they have filled. I have heard how kind you have been to Naomi. And how you left your own people to come here with her. May God himself reward you.'

That night, when she went home, Ruth told Naomi what had happened. Naomi was very pleased. She knew that Boaz was a good man. And she wanted Ruth to marry again.

In Israel in those days, when a man died, his closest relative had to take care of the dead man's family. Naomi wanted to claim this right, and ask Boaz to marry Ruth.

She knew that Boaz was spending the night at the threshing-floor, to make sure no one stole his corn. So she sent Ruth to see him, secretly, after dark.

'Tell Naomi I agree,' Boaz said to Ruth. 'I will marry you. But there is a man who is a closer relative than I am. I must see him about it first.'

Next day Boaz met the man who was Naomi's closest relative at the town gate. This man had a family of his own and did not want to marry Ruth. So the matter was settled.

Boaz married Ruth.

And when Ruth had a son, there was no happier woman in Bethlehem than Naomi.

Hannah's baby

In the village of Ramah, in the hills near Jerusalem,
lived a man called Elkanah. He had two wives—
Penninah, who had many sons and daughters, and
Hannah, who had no children at all. Hannah was sad
about this, although she knew that her husband loved
her very much.

Every year Elkanah took his family to Shiloh to
worship God. Afterwards they had a celebration meal
together, in God's house. And Penninah, who was
surrounded by her children, taunted Hannah who was
all alone and made her more unhappy than ever.

When the meal was over, Hannah moved away
from the others. She cried her heart out, telling God
just how miserable she was.

'If you give me a son,' she said, 'I promise he will
serve you all his life.'

And God heard, as he always hears.

But Eli the priest, who had been watching her,
thought she was drunk.

'Please don't think unkindly of me,' she said. 'I am
not drunk—but I am very unhappy.' And she told him
all about it.

Then Eli said to her,

'Go in peace. And may God give you the son you long for.'

So Hannah dried her eyes and went home comforted.

And God answered her prayer. He gave her a beautiful baby boy whom she called Samuel.

'As soon as he is old enough I will take him to Shiloh to serve God,' she said. 'He will stay there all his life, as I promised.'

And she did as she said.

'This is the son I prayed for,' she said to Eli the priest. 'God gave him to me. And now I am giving him back to God. Please take care of him and train him for God's work.'

A few days later the family went home to Ramah, leaving Samuel with Eli. God knew how hard it was for Hannah to part with her little son, and as time went by he gave her three more sons and two daughters to love and care for.

Once a year, when they went to Shiloh, Hannah saw Samuel. She took him the new clothes she had made him. He was growing into a fine boy, and everyone loved him.

Eli was by now an old man. Soon his sons would take charge of God's house. But Eli's sons were not like their father. They were greedy men with no love or respect for God. God warned Eli that he would not allow men like this to serve him as priests.

'I will choose a priest who will be loyal to me and do all I want,' he said.

One night, Samuel was sleeping in God's house. He woke with a start. Someone was calling his name! Samuel ran to Eli, but the old priest had not called him.

It happened again.

'You called me. Here I am,' he said. But Eli had not called. Then the old priest knew it must be God who was calling Samuel's name.

So when the voice called a third time, 'Samuel! Samuel!' the boy answered as Eli had told him.

'Speak; your servant is listening.'

'I am going to punish Eli's sons,' God said. 'None of his family shall ever be my priests again.'

Next morning, when Eli asked what God had said, Samuel did not want to tell him. But the old man made him speak. Sadly he listened to the boy's story.

'Let God do what seems good to him,' he said.

Some time later the people of Israel were at war with the Philistines. The Israelites were losing, so they sent to Shiloh for the special box which held God's law. They thought it would bring them luck in battle! Eli's two sons brought it to the camp.

But it did them no good. The Philistines won a great victory. They captured the sacred box and killed Eli's sons.

Eli was very old by now, and almost blind. When he heard the terrible news he had a fall and broke his neck.

The Philistines returned to their city of Ashdod in triumph. They put the sacred box in the temple of Dagon their god, as a trophy of war.

Next day, Dagon's statue was lying flat on its face before the box.

They lifted it back into place, but the following morning, there it was again—this time smashed to pieces.

Then plague broke out in the city, and the people were really afraid.

'This is the work of Israel's God,' they said. 'Let's get rid of the sacred box.'

So they sent it to the city of Gath—and from Gath to Ekron—and plague broke out there, too. The Philistines were worried and confused. They consulted their priests and magicians.

'Send the box back to Israel with a present for God,' these wise men advised. 'Then you will be healed. Remember what God did to the Egyptians!'

So they put the box on a cart and harnessed two cows to pull it. Then they watched to see what would happen. The cows behaved like a trained team of oxen! Straight across the border they went, to Bethshemesh in Israel. How the villagers rejoiced to see the sacred box of God return!

Then the Philistines knew that the God of Israel was a God to be respected.

Samuel, the king-maker

Eli was dead. God had chosen Samuel to teach the
people of Israel his ways, and to be his priest. Samuel
loved God and obeyed him.

But Samuel's sons were no better than Eli's sons
had been. They were greedy and dishonest. So the
people came to Samuel.

'You are growing old,' they said. 'And we do not
want your sons to lead us. Give us a king, like the other
nations.'

Samuel was not at all pleased about this. And
neither was God! He was the real King of Israel—the
one who had saved them from Egypt and given them
good laws. Now they were rejecting his rule.

'You want a king, like the other nations,' Samuel
said. 'But this is what your king will do to you. He will
make your sons soldiers in his army. You will have to
farm the land for him, and make his weapons. He will
take your best cattle and crops and land. And you will
become his slaves. That is what kings are like. You will
be sorry you ever asked for a king.'

But the people said, 'No.' They wanted a king to
rule them and lead them into battle.

So God said,

'Do what they want. Give them a king.'

Israel's first king was a fine, tall, good-looking man
called Saul. He was out searching for his father's lost
donkeys when Samuel first met him. And God said to
Samuel,

'This is the man who will rule my people.'

So Samuel did what was the custom in those days.

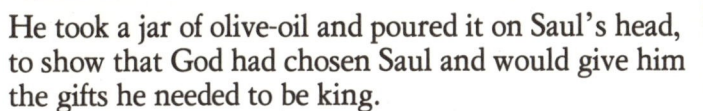

He took a jar of olive-oil and poured it on Saul's head, to show that God had chosen Saul and would give him the gifts he needed to be king.

And at first Saul was a good king. He was brave. He led his people into battle, and won wars. And he was very popular. But then he began to grow proud and obstinate. He would not listen to Samuel. He would not do as God said.

There came a day when God said to Samuel, 'Saul is no longer fit to be king. I have chosen his successor. Go to Bethlehem and anoint the new king— he is one of the sons of Jesse. But keep it a secret.'

Samuel was very sad for Saul. But he knew Saul would not change. So he went to Bethlehem. He said he had come to make a special offering to God. And he invited Jesse and his sons to the feast.

Jesse came, with seven sons, all of them tall and strong and good-looking. Samuel spoke to each of them in turn, and every time he thought to himself,

'Surely this is the man God has chosen.'

But each time, God said no!

'Don't be taken in by good looks,' God said. 'I judge by what a person is like inside—if he is good and loving and kind.'

'Have you any more sons?' Samuel asked Jesse.

'Yes,' Jesse answered, 'the youngest. But he is out looking after the sheep.'

'Tell him to come,' Samuel said. 'We can't begin the feast until he's here.'

So Jesse sent for David.

And when David walked in, God said to Samuel, 'This is the one!'

Samuel took the olive-oil he had brought with him and he poured it on David's head.

After the feast, Samuel went home.

And David continued to look after his father's sheep, out on the hills around Bethlehem. But God was with David in a special way, from that day on.

The shepherd boy and the giant

All day long, David was out on the hills looking after his father's sheep. Sometimes one of them strayed and he went after it and brought it back. Sometimes a hungry jackal—even a bear or a lion—tried to carry off one of the flock. Then David needed all his strength and skill to beat the wild animal off and rescue the sheep.

But most of the time there was little or nothing to do, except move the sheep on now and then to better pasture—a new place, where the grass was thick and green.

But David wasn't bored. He practised with his sling until he was a crack shot. And he played his harp, often singing songs he made up for himself. He began to get quite a name as a musician! People stopped to listen. This boy's playing was something special.

Meanwhile there was trouble in the palace. King Saul was an unhappy man. Samuel never came to him these days. God was far away. Everything was going wrong. Saul's black moods came more and more often. Something had to be done.

'What the king needs is music,' one of his servants said, 'to calm him down and make him forget his troubles.'

'I know just the man,' said another.

And that was how David first came to the king's palace. His music worked better than any medicine. Saul's troubled mind was set at rest. Soon he was well again, and David was sent back home.

News came that the Philistines, the old enemies of Israel, were marching north. They set up camp in the Valley of Elah. The Philistine army was on one side of the valley, the Israelite army on the other—and a little brook ran between them.

The Philistines had a secret weapon! His name was Goliath—a great giant of a man, ten feet tall. The shaft of his spear was as thick as a man's arm. Day after day Goliath walked proudly to and fro, shouting and jeering.

'Where is the champion of Israel? Let him come out and fight me, if he dare!'

But no one did. They were all much too afraid.

Three of David's brothers were soldiers in Saul's army, and David was sent with food, to see how they were. He arrived one day, just in time to hear Goliath's threats.

'Who is this man,' said David, 'to defy the armies of the living God? Let *me* go and fight him.'

The soldiers only laughed. But when Saul heard of it he sent for David.

'You are just a boy,' he said. 'What chance do you have against this great warrior?'

'I have fought lions and bears that attacked the sheep,' said David. 'God was with me then. He will be with me now.'

'Very well,' said the king. 'Go. And God be with you.'

He gave David his sword and dressed him up in his own armour. But David couldn't even walk in it!

'I can't fight with all this on,' he said. And he took it off again.

He picked up his shepherd's stick and his sling. He chose five smooth stones from the brook and put them in his bag. Then he went out to fight Goliath.

When Goliath saw him coming, he laughed till his sides ached.

'Is this your champion?' he jeered at the Israelites.

But David said,

'Today God will give you into my hand. Then everyone will know that there is a God in Israel.'

He took a stone from his bag and fitted it into his sling. The stone flew like a rocket. It hit Goliath on the forehead with such force it pierced his skull.

David ran up to him, took Goliath's sword from its sheath, and cut off the giant's head.

The Philistine army gave a great cry—then they all turned and ran—with the Israelites in hot pursuit.

The battle was won.

David and the king's son

David's victory over Goliath made him famous. Saul took him to stay at the palace.

'He shall marry my daughter,' the king said.

Saul's son, Jonathan, took an instant liking to David. Soon they were firm friends. They promised one another they'd be friends for ever, no matter what might happen.

David joined the army and became a great soldier. He was very popular. The people sang his praises—and Saul grew jealous. David was engaged to Saul's daughter, Merab. But the king put off the wedding.

One day, as David sat playing his harp, Saul hurled a spear at him. And this was only the beginning of the trouble.

Saul made Merab marry another man, breaking his promise to David. And when he heard that Michal, his younger daughter, was in love with David, he saw his chance to get David killed.

'No need for a wedding-gift,' he said. 'All I want is 200 dead Philistines!' It was a clever idea. Saul was sure the Philistines would kill David. But instead David and his men carried out the king's order and David married Michal.

Jonathan hated all this plotting. He warned David that Saul was out to get him killed, and he pleaded with the king to change his mind and spare David. Saul agreed. But again he broke his word.

As David was playing his harp one evening, Saul's spear whistled past his head, and stuck quivering in the wall. Life in the palace was no longer safe.

That night Michal helped David escape by shinning down a rope from the window of their house, when the guards were not looking. Jonathan and David said a very sad goodbye. They were never to meet again.

From then on, David was an outlaw living in the hills. He gathered a band of men and they moved from place to place, finding what food they could. Danger was never far away. Sometimes Saul's men were so close that escape seemed impossible. But God was still with David, keeping him safe till the time came for him to become king.

Once Saul came alone and unarmed to the entrance of the cave where David and his men were hiding. The king was at his mercy. But David refused to harm him.

Several times people told the king where David was hiding, and Saul came to hunt him out. He camped near Ziph, once, with his army. And at dead of night David and two of his men crept past the guard to the place where Saul lay sleeping, with his spear stuck in the ground beside him.

'Kill him now, and end your troubles,' whispered David's men. 'God has given him to you.'

But David said, 'I will never harm the man God chose as king. Let him die in God's own good time.'

No one saw them leave the camp, taking Saul's spear and water-jar with them. When they were a good way off, David gave a great shout that woke the camp with a start.

'Fine guards you are!' he said. 'You should take better care of the king. Look, here is his spear!'

Saul knew that voice. It was David's. And David had spared his life. Saul was ashamed that he had treated David so badly. And for a while he left him alone. But not for long.

Nowhere in Israel was really safe, now. So David took refuge in the Philistine city of Ziklag. He pretended to be on the side of the Philistines.

He was there when the Philistines marched north to wage war on Israel. They camped near Shunem, and a terrible battle took place on the mountains of Gilboa.

Jonathan died that day, with the rest of Saul's sons. The king was so badly wounded that he fell on his own sword, rather than be taken alive by the enemy.

Next day, when they found him, the Philistines cut off his head and fastened his body to the wall at Bethshan. But brave men came and took it down, and gave the king proper burial.

The whole nation mourned.

David was full of sorrow when he heard the news. He lifted his voice in a great lament:

'Saul and Jonathan, beloved and lovely!

In life and in death they were not divided.

How are the mighty fallen in the midst of battle.'

And David cried until he could cry no more.

Long live King David!

The trumpets sounded. The people gave a great shout.

'David is being crowned king of Israel. Long live King David!'

The days as an outlaw were over. But that was not the end of David's troubles. The followers of the old king— Saul—fought against him. The Philistines and other old enemies were always waiting to return. And at the heart of his kingdom the fortress of Jerusalem was still held by a Canaanite tribe.

It was a great day when David stormed the stronghold and made the city of Jerusalem his new capital.

There was peace at last. Now David could do something he had wanted to do for a long time. He gave orders for the sacred box which held God's law to be brought to Jerusalem.

What a day of singing and dancing and feasting that was! And King David outdanced them all—he was so full of joy. Now Jerusalem was more than his own capital city. It was the city of God!

David was a good king—a great soldier and statesman; a born leader. He had many sons and daughters. All his people loved him. He did not grow proud and disobedient as King Saul had done. He remained loyal to God all his life. But there were times, even so, when things went badly wrong.

The poor man's lamb

One afternoon in spring, when his army was away fighting a tribe called the Ammonites, King David went on to the flat roof of the palace, where the air was cooler. Glancing down, he saw the most beautiful woman he had ever seen.

'Who is that?' he asked.

'Bathsheba, Uriah's wife,' came the reply.

Now Uriah was one of David's bravest soldiers, and he was away fighting the king's war. But David put all that out of his mind. He ordered his servants to bring

Bathsheba to the palace, and he made love to her.

A few weeks later, Bathsheba sent to tell the king she was going to have a baby—David's child. What would happen when Uriah, her husband, found out? David had to act quickly. He sent the order to his army commander:

'Send Uriah to the front line, and make sure he is killed.'

It was all done in secret. No one else knew—or so David thought. But he was forgetting about God.

Uriah died.

David married Bathsheba.

The child—a boy—was born.

David thought his secret would never be known.

And then one day a man called Nathan, God's messenger, came to the king with a story.

'Once upon a time,' he began, 'there were two men —one very rich, the other very poor. The rich man owned great flocks and herds. The poor man had only one lamb—it was almost like one of the family. The rich man had a visitor, and needed a lamb for the meal. But, instead of killing one of his own flock, he took the poor man's lamb, killed it, cooked it and gave it to his guest to eat.'

The story made David very angry indeed. How could anyone be so cruel? There was a long silence. Then Nathan spoke again, and his words were sharp as arrows.

'*You* are the man,' he said. 'God made you king and gave you all you could wish for. Yet you took Uriah's wife, and sent him to his death. God saw it all. Don't think that just because you are king you can do a thing like that and get away with it. Because of your sin the child will die.'

David was horrified—and bitterly sorry for the wrong he had done. But he could not save the child's life. The boy died.

David comforted Bathsheba, and God forgave him and gave them a second son. They called him Solomon.

The king was busy and active in the years that followed. He fought many battles and his kingdom grew strong. But he wanted, more than anything, to build a special house, a temple, for God. However, this was not to be.

'That is something for Solomon to do,' God said.

So David had to be content with drawing up the plans and storing up gold and silver, bronze, iron and wood, and precious stones—ready for Solomon to start building. And he spent many hours arranging the temple services, especially the music. For David loved music and wrote a great many hymns.[*]

Rebellion

Yes, David was certainly a great king—one of the greatest. But within his own family it was a different story. He could manage state affairs—but he could not control his own sons. And he paid dearly for his weakness.

---

[*]Some of David's songs are in the book of Psalms, in the Bible.

All the people loved the king's good-looking young
son, Absalom. But being loved was not enough for him.
Absalom had set his heart on becoming king. He
plotted against his father and arranged a meeting at
Hebron, where he was proclaimed king. Then he
marched on the capital city, Jerusalem, and David was
forced to run for his life.

It was civil war.

Ahithophel, the wisest of all David's advisers, went
over to Absalom's side—and things looked black for
the king. But God had not forgotten him. He loved
David and had taken care of him all his life. And he was
still looking after him.

Hushai, David's trusted friend, pretended to side
with Absalom, when he was really sending secret
information about Absalom's plans to the king.

Instead of following David and taking him by
surprise (as Ahithophel advised), Absalom let Hushai
persuade him to wait. This gave David the time he
needed to gather his army.

There was a terrible battle, and David's army won.
Absalom escaped as fast as he could. But he rode his
mule under a low-spreading tree, and was caught in the
branches. There David's soldiers found him. And
against the king's express orders to spare Absalom's
life, they killed him.

When David heard the news, he felt he could not bear it.

'Oh, my son Absalom,' he sobbed. 'How I wish I had died instead of you. Oh, Absalom, my son!'

So the great day of victory ended in mourning.

David returned to Jerusalem and punished the rebels. There were no more threats to his throne. But after Absalom's rebellion and death the king began to feel old and tired. And the people began to ask which of David's sons would be the next king of Israel.

Solomon the wise

King David had grown old and weak, and there was trouble about who should succeed him as king. With Absalom dead, David's next son, Adonijah, claimed the throne.

But David had other plans. He sent for Zadok the priest, Nathan the prophet and Benaiah the captain of the guard.

'Solomon is to be king when I die,' David said. 'He is to ride on my own mule to the Spring of Gihon. Zadok and Nathan will anoint him king. Then you must blow the trumpet and shout, "Long live King Solomon".'

So Zadok, Nathan, Benaiah and the king's guard did as David said. Solomon was proclaimed king. The trumpets were blown. And all the people shouted,

'Long live King Solomon!'

Then they brought him back to the city, playing their flutes and shouting for joy.

David gave Solomon his last command.

'Be a strong king,' he said. 'Follow God and keep his commands—and all will be well. If you obey him, God will keep the promise he made me that my descendants will always rule this nation.'

So King David died, and King Solomon reigned in the royal city—God's city—of Jerusalem. Solomon ruled over the kingdom of Israel, a strong and united kingdom. And he loved God as his father had done.

One night, God came to Solomon in a dream.

'What would you like me to give you?' God said.

'I am very young,' Solomon answered. 'And I have to rule all these people. Please make me wise, so that I can rule justly and do what is right.'

God was pleased that Solomon had wanted wisdom more than riches or fame.

'I will make you the wisest of all men,' he said. 'And I will also give you riches and fame.'

As God had promised, Solomon became the wisest of men—wiser than all the wise men of the East; wiser than all the wise men of Egypt.

King Solomon composed 3,000 proverbs!* But he never forgot that wisdom comes from God. It is not the same as simply being clever. No one can be truly wise unless they respect God and listen to what he says.

The queen of Sheba

Solomon's fame spread far and wide. Merchants carried tales of his wisdom across the desert to the land of Sheba. The queen of Sheba didn't really believe what they said, but she was curious to find out for herself what this king was like.

She made a list of all the hardest questions she could think of, to test him. Then she set out on the long

*Some of them are in the book of Proverbs, in the Bible.

journey, with all her attendants, and camels loaded with rare spices, jewels and gold.

The people of Jerusalem were used to seeing foreign visitors. But they stopped and stared when the queen of Sheba arrived!

The queen was shown into the palace. She asked King Solomon every question on her list—and he answered them all! She was shown round the palace. She saw the food that was prepared for the king's table, and his great feasts. She saw the palace officials in their splendid uniforms. It quite took her breath away!

'I didn't believe what they told me about you,' she said to the king. 'But now I have seen for myself. God has given his people a wise king because he loves them.'

She gave King Solomon the gifts she had brought with her: rare spices, jewels and gold. The king gave her gifts of his own in exchange—and anything else she cared to ask for. Then the queen and her attendants returned to the land of Sheba.

Solomon builds a house for God

When Solomon had been king for four years, he began to build a house for God—the Temple.

Great stones were cut from the quarries for the foundations and the walls. Solomon also needed cedar-wood. The very best cedars grew, not in Israel, but in the land of King Hiram of Tyre, to the north. So King Solomon and King Hiram made a treaty. The cedars were felled and brought down to the sea. The logs were tied together to make rafts, and floated down the coast.

The Temple was not very big, but it was as beautiful as King Solomon could make it. There were two rooms: the main one was oblong, and the inner room was square, with a double door between them.

The inner room had no windows, so it was quite dark inside. It held the box with the law of God. And above it were two huge beasts with outstretched wings made of olive-wood covered with gold. This was God's special room. No one ever went in—except the high priest, just once a year on the Day of Atonement.

In the outer room there was an altar, and ten lampstands. It was not like a church or a cathedral. The people did not go inside. It was God's house.

The walls of the Temple were lined from floor to ceiling with cedar panels. These were decorated with carvings of winged beasts, palm-trees and flowers. The whole of the inside of the Temple was covered with gold—even the pine floor.

Outside the Temple there were courtyards where the people could bring animals for the priests to kill and offer to God.

A famous craftsman from Tyre came to cast the two bronze pillars at the entrance to the Temple; and a vast bronze tank which rested on the backs of twelve bronze bulls; and ten ornate bronze stands on wheels, holding basins.

It took many workmen seven long years to build and furnish God's Temple. But at last it was done. How beautiful it looked. Nothing but the very best for God.

Then Solomon gathered all the people together.
The priests made special offerings to God. They
brought the sacred box containing God's law, and put it
in the inner room—and the glory of God's presence
filled the Temple.

Solomon stood before the people.

'O Lord, God of Israel,' he prayed, 'there is no
other God like you, who loves his people and keeps all
his promises. Watch over your Temple. Hear the
prayers of your people. Forgive them and help them
always.'

Then he turned to the people.

'May God be with us, as he was with our fathers,'
he said. 'Be true to God and obey all his commands.'

After the ceremony, they held a great feast, lasting
a whole week. Then the people went home.

Trouble

King Solomon's reign was a 'golden age' for Israel. His merchants traded far and wide and grew rich. He built ships and they brought back precious cargoes. Fine new buildings sprang up, and great fortress cities were built.

But not everything was good. More and more money and men were needed for the building work. The people had to pay taxes. And the men were forced to work for the king instead of on their own farms.

King Solomon married many foreign princesses. It was good for trade and there was peace. But the princesses brought their own gods with them. They did not worship God. And when he was old, Solomon let his wives persuade him to worship their gods. He was no longer loyal to God, as his father David had been.

God spoke to Solomon:

'Because you have not kept my commands, the kingdom will be taken from your son.'

God's words came true.

Solomon died. And not long after, the kingdom of Israel divided into two parts. Judah, the southern part, stayed loyal to Solomon's son, King Rehoboam. But the ten northern tribes broke away and made Jeroboam, one of King Solomon's officials, their king. Jeroboam made two gold bulls for God's people to worship. He placed one at Bethel, in the south, the other at Dan, in the north. He wanted to stop the people going to God's Temple in Jerusalem. But what he did was wrong. It led to terrible trouble.

Elijah and the prophets of Baal

Jeroboam was the first king of the northern kingdom of Israel. Not one of the kings of Israel who followed him was loyal to God. They all encouraged the people to worship the bull idols Jeroboam had made.

Ahab, the seventh king, was even worse than the others. He married a cruel and wicked queen—Jezebel, the king of Sidon's daughter. And he built a special temple for Baal, the god of war and weather worshipped by Jezebel and her people.

Queen Jezebel killed many of God's prophets—men who taught the people to love and obey him. But there

was still one man in Ahab's kingdom who spoke out boldly for God—the prophet Elijah.

One day God said to Elijah,

'Go and tell King Ahab that I know all the terrible things he has done. Tell him there will be no rain in Israel until I give the word.'

Elijah delivered God's message. Then God sent him to stay in a safe place on the far side of the River Jordan, by Cherith Brook. Elijah drank water from the brook, and every day God sent ravens to bring him food.

But after a while the brook dried up because there was no rain. God said to Elijah:

'Go north to Zarephath near Sidon. There is a widow there who will give you food.'

Elijah did as he was told. As he came to the town he met a widow picking up sticks.

'Please bring me a drink of water,' he said, 'and some bread to eat.'

'I have no bread,' she answered. 'All I have left is a handful of flour and a few drops of olive-oil. I'm going to take these sticks home and bake a last meal. Then my son and I must starve.'

'Don't worry,' said Elijah. 'Bake a small loaf for me first. God says your flour and oil will not run out till the drought is over.'

The woman did as Elijah said. And she found that he was right. The flour and the oil did not run out. Day after day she baked bread—and there was always just enough flour and just enough oil.

But one day the widow's son fell ill. He got worse and worse, and then he died.

'What have you done?' the woman said to Elijah. 'Is this some kind of punishment? Have you reminded God of the wrong things I've done?' She was terribly upset.

'Give the boy to me,' Elijah answered. Then he carried the boy upstairs to the room where he was staying and laid him on the bed.

Elijah prayed out loud to God. 'You know how kind the widow has been to me,' he said. 'Please bring her son back to life.'

Three times he prayed to God. And God brought the child back to life.

The widow could hardly believe it. She took the boy in her arms and turned to the prophet:

'Now I know that you really are a man of God, and speak the truth,' she said.

The challenge

There was no rain for three years and the people were starving.

Then God told Elijah to go and see King Ahab.

'Why have you come?' the king said. 'You are the worst troublemaker in Israel.'

'That is not true,' said Elijah. 'You are the one who has brought trouble on Israel, by disobeying God and worshipping Baal. Now tell all the people and the prophets of Baal to meet me on Mount Carmel.'

The king did as he said.

When everyone was there, Elijah spoke to them.

'It is time you made up your minds,' he said. 'You can't worship Baal *and* God. Let's see which is the true God. If the Lord is God, worship him. But if Baal is god, worship him.'

Then he turned to the prophets of Baal.

'Let us both offer a sacrifice. You offer a bull to Baal, and I will offer a bull to God. The god who answers by fire is the true God.'

So the priests of Baal made an altar. They put wood on the altar and killed their bull. Then they laid the bull on top of the wood.

All day long they called out, 'Baal, hear us!' They worked themselves into a great frenzy—but there was no reply. Nothing happened.

When Elijah's turn came, he built an altar, put wood on top and killed his bull. Then he poured water over the dead body of his bull, soaking the wood. And he dug a ditch round the altar and filled it with water.

'O Lord God of Israel,' he prayed, 'let the people see that you are God.'

Then God sent fire down. Fierce flames licked up the water and burnt the offering.

When they saw it, the people threw themselves face down on the ground.

'The Lord, he is God! The Lord, he is God!' they shouted. They seized all the prophets of Baal before they could escape, and killed them.

Then Elijah asked God for rain. In a little while the wind blew, the sky grew dark, and rain began to fall. It was the greatest day of Elijah's life. He felt on top of the world. He even ran in front of the king's chariot all the way to the palace at Jezreel.

But next day everything had changed. Elijah was running again—but this time for his life. Queen Jezebel had sworn to kill him. On and on he went, mile after mile, south till he came to the desert, and on again till he reached Mount Sinai.

He was completely alone. Everything was quiet—not a sound to be heard. And then God's voice came to him.

'What are you doing here, Elijah?'

'They have killed all your prophets,' he said miserably. 'I am the only one left—and they want to kill me, too.'

'Go back,' God said to him, 'there is still work for you to do. Leave Queen Jezebel and King Ahab to me. Go and find Elisha, who is to be my prophet after you. And don't think you are alone. There are still 7,000 people in Israel who have never worshipped Baal.'

So Elijah took courage. He found Elisha at work in the fields, ploughing. He took off his cloak and put it around Elisha's shoulders—to show that he was to be the next prophet in Israel. And Elisha left home and went with him.

King Ahab and the vineyard

Next to King Ahab's palace at Jezreel there was a vineyard. It belonged to a man called Naboth.

'That vineyard would make a wonderful vegetable garden,' thought the king.

So he called Naboth to him and asked if he would sell it, or if he would agree to take another vineyard in exchange. But Naboth was firm.

'Oh no,' he said. 'That vineyard has always belonged to my family. I want to leave it to my son when I die. And God's law forbids me to sell it to someone else.'

King Ahab was used to getting his own way. People did not say 'No' to him! Naboth's answer made him angry. He sulked.

He was in such a bad mood that Queen Jezebel asked him what was the matter.

'Aren't you the king?' she said, when he explained. 'You shall have that vineyard. Leave it to me.'

Queen Jezebel always got what she wanted. It didn't matter how, or who got hurt.

She had Naboth accused of treason, convicted and stoned to death. (He was quite innocent, of course.) Then she went to the king.

'Naboth is dead,' she said. 'There's nothing to stop you taking his vineyard now.'

The king was down at the vineyard when Elijah the prophet came to see him.

'God says that because you spilt the blood of Naboth, your own blood will be spilt. Jezebel will die here in Jezreel. And your whole family will be destroyed.'

Ahab was horrified at Elijah's words. For a time he changed his ways. But it didn't last.

Three years later, King Ahab joined forces with King Jehoshaphat of Judah and went to war against the Syrians. There was a great battle at Ramoth-gilead.

Jehoshaphat dressed in his royal robes, as usual. Ahab thought he would be safer in disguise, and dressed as an ordinary soldier. But one of the enemy archers drew his bow—and his arrow found a gap in the king's armour. Ahab bled to death in his chariot.

God had kept his word.

Stories of Elisha

Elijah was old now, and the time came for him to make his last journey. Elisha, as always, went with him.

A group of prophets followed them from Jericho and stood watching as they reached the River Jordan. Elijah rolled up his cloak and struck the water. A path opened in front of them and the two men walked across.

On the far side, Elijah said to Elisha,

'I shall be leaving you very soon. Is there anything you want, before I go?'

'I shall have to carry on your work without you,' Elisha answered. 'I am your heir—leave me your power.'

'That is a hard thing to do,' Elijah replied. 'But if you see me when I'm taken from you, then you can be sure you will be given what you've asked for.'

They were still talking when a flaming chariot drawn by fiery horses swept between them. And Elisha saw Elijah caught up to heaven in a great rush of wind. He was left alone.

Sadly he picked up Elijah's cloak and returned to the river. He struck the water, saying,

'Where is the Lord, the God of Elijah?'

And the waters parted, as before, for him to cross. Then the watching prophets knew they would never see Elijah again, and that God had chosen Elisha to take his place.

The house at Shunem

As God's prophet in Israel, Elisha travelled a great deal, going from place to place teaching God's law.

One day he arrived at Shunem, feeling hungry and dusty and tired. As he passed her door, a rich woman invited him in for a meal.

'Come back whenever you like,' she said, as he left.

Elisha liked the woman—she was as kind as she was rich. And after that he often came to the house.

Then the woman said to her husband,

'Let's build this man of God a room of his own. Then he can stay here and rest whenever he comes to Shunem.'

They built the room on the flat roof of the house. And when it was finished, the woman put a bed in it, and a table, a chair and a lamp. Elisha was delighted.

'These people have done so much for us,' he said to his servant Gehazi. 'Is there anything we can do in return?'

'They are rich,' said Gehazi. 'They have everything they could want—except a child.'

So Elisha called the woman to him.

'This time next year you will have a son,' he said. And to her joy, Elisha's words came true.

But some years later, tragedy struck. The little boy

was helping his father with the harvest, when he suddenly cried out, 'My head hurts! My head hurts!' His father sent him home to his mother. But within a few hours he was dead.

The boy's mother carried him up to Elisha's room and shut the door. Then she had the donkey saddled, and set off to find Elisha and bring him back.

When Elisha reached Shunem, he went into the room alone, and saw the boy lying dead on the bed.

'O Lord God,' Elisha prayed, 'give back the child's life.'

He put his mouth to the child's mouth—and the boy's body started to grow warm.

The boy sneezed seven times, and opened his eyes.

'Come quickly,' Elisha called to the woman. 'Your son is alive and well!'

The Syrian commander

Naaman was a great man in Syria—the commander of the king's army. He had everything a man could want—power, fame, riches, a big house and servants to wait on him. But he also had a terrible skin disease and in those days there was no cure. He and his wife were most upset.

On one of their raids, the Syrians had captured a little Israelite girl. And she had become a servant to Naaman's wife.

'There is a prophet at home in Israel who could heal the master,' she said.

So the king of Syria arranged safe-conduct, and Naaman went to Israel to find Elisha.

Elisha's servant answered the door.

'My master says you are to go and wash seven times in the River Jordan,' he said, 'and you will be cured.'

What a let-down! Naaman had expected Elisha to do something dramatic. He was very annoyed.

'There are better rivers in Syria, if all I have to do is wash,' he said. But his servants persuaded him to try, all the same. And it worked. He went to the river, waded in, and ducked down into the water seven times. And he was completely cured!

He hurried back to thank the prophet.

'Now I know that the God of Israel is the only true God,' he said.

God's army

War broke out again between Syria and Israel. The Syrians had set up an ambush. But Elisha warned the king of Israel not to go near the place. Every time the Syrians made a plan, Elisha knew and warned the king of Israel.

'Find Elisha and take him captive,' roared the king of Syria.

News came that Elisha was at Dothan.

The king of Syria sent horses and chariots by night to surround the town. Next morning, Elisha's servant was in a panic when he saw them.

'We're trapped,' he said to Elisha. 'Whatever shall we do?'

But Elisha wasn't worried at all.

'O Lord God,' he prayed, 'open my servant's eyes.'

The servant looked up and this time he saw a host of fiery horses and chariots surrounding the Syrian army. And he knew that God was protecting his prophet from harm.

Elisha did a great many wonderful things in his lifetime. He became so famous that kings came to ask his advice. But he always had time to help ordinary people. And when he died, the whole nation mourned.

Joash—the boy king

In the northern kingdom of Israel (where Elijah and Elisha lived) there was a constant struggle for power. The kings were not loyal to God. And there were wars and rebellions.

Things were better in Judah, the southern kingdom. In Jerusalem, the capital city, one king after another came to the throne, all of them belonging to the family line of King David. Most of them were good kings, loyal to God. But some were like the kings of Israel. They turned away from the living God to worship Baal and other gods, who were really only idols.

After Solomon came his son, King Rehoboam; after Rehoboam, his son King Abijah;

. . . and *his* son, King Asa;

. . . and *his* son, King Jehoshaphat;

. . . and *his* son, King Jehoram.

King Jehoram did a silly thing. He married Athaliah, the daughter of King Ahab of Israel. He should have known that a marriage like that would lead to trouble. And it did. But the worst of it came after King Jehoram had died.

The new king, Ahaziah (the son of King Jehoram and Queen Athaliah) decided to go on a family visit to the king of Israel. Unluckily he chose the wrong time.

While he was there an army officer called Jehu led a revolt. The king of Israel was killed. And Jezebel (the queen mother) was thrown from the palace window at Jezreel to die a horrible death (as God had said she would).

Ahaziah leapt into his chariot and tried to escape. But Jehu's men caught up with him, and he was so badly wounded he died before he could get home.

When Queen Athaliah heard what had happened she went mad with rage. She ordered her soldiers to kill every single member of the royal family. She would rule the kingdom of Judah herself.

That would have been the end of King David's family line. But God had made a promise to King David: 'Your dynasty will never end.'

Athaliah killed all the royal family—except one. King Ahaziah's baby son, Joash, was rescued by his aunt, who took him to the Temple and hid him there.

For six years Joash was looked after by the high priest, Jehoiada. It was a complete secret. No one knew.

But when Joash was seven, Jehoiada sent for the soldiers in command of the royal guard and let them into the secret.

'This is what you must do,' he said. And he told them his plan.

The following Saturday, the Sabbath, all the guards who were going off duty went straight to the Temple.

Then Jehoiada led Joash out of the Temple, with the guards all around him, swords drawn. He put the crown on the boy's head and proclaimed him the true king of Judah.

The people were overjoyed.

'Long live the king!' they shouted.

When Queen Athaliah heard the noise she hurried to the Temple and saw Joash standing there.

'Treason! Treason!' she shouted.

But no one came to help her. Queen Athaliah's reign had been a reign of terror. Everyone feared and hated her. So the soldiers took her away, and killed her.

Then the people went to the temple of Baal and tore down the idols and smashed the altars. Now they were free once again to worship God and live in peace.

Joash reigned for forty years. Jehoiada, the high priest, had taught him to know and love God's law from his babyhood. And he did not forget it.

God's Temple had been neglected. The first thing Joash wanted to do as king was to repair and restore it. So Joash became famous in history not only as the boy king, but as the king who repaired God's Temple.

Invasion from the north

About seventy years after the death of King Joash, his great-great-great grandson Hezekiah came to the throne of Judah. Hezekiah had problems.

The kingdom of Assyria, to the north-east, had grown in power. Assyrian soldiers poured across the borders into neighbouring countries. They stormed cities. They plundered. They killed. Stories of their terrible cruelty made everyone afraid.

One by one the smaller kingdoms around were swallowed up into the great Assyrian Empire.

Hezekiah had been king four years when the Assyrians marched south into Israel. For nearly three years they besieged Samaria, the capital city of the northern kingdom. Many people starved to death before the city fell.

The Assyrians took the king of Israel prisoner.
They forced the Israelites to leave their own country
and march weary miles to a far-off land. They never
came home again.

Foreigners were brought into the land of Israel.
They settled in Samaria, bringing their own gods with
them.

It was a terrible thing to happen. And all because
the Israelites refused to listen to God or to obey him.
Time and time again he had warned them. But they had
simply turned a deaf ear.

Things were not much better in Judah. The people worshipped images made of wood and stone. God was almost forgotten.

But the people of Judah were lucky: they had Hezekiah as their king. And Hezekiah was a good man, who trusted God. He ordered the images to be taken down and smashed.

'I want my people to trust God, as I do,' he said.

The people of Judah were lucky for another reason, too: they had Isaiah as their prophet. And Isaiah told them what was in God's mind.

'Don't be like the people of Israel,' he said. 'You can see where it leads. Love God and obey him. The Assyrians are coming. But don't be afraid. God is with us.'

Just seven years later, the Assyrians did come. They marched south into Judah and attacked the fortresses on the border. Nearer and nearer they came—until they were at the gates of Jerusalem itself. They had King Hezekiah and Isaiah and all the people shut up inside like birds in a cage.

Three of the Assyrian army chiefs stood at the city gates. They shouted for the king—and three of Hezekiah's councillors went out to them. The people of Jerusalem watched and listened from the city wall. They shivered with fright as the sun caught the bright metal of the spears and shields of row upon row of Assyrian soldiers.

'These are the words of Sennacherib, the great king of Assyria,' the Assyrians said. 'Make peace while you can. You are in my power. Do you think your God can save you? Did the gods of all the other countries save them from our king? Did anyone save Samaria? Don't let Hezekiah fool you into thinking God will rescue you. Come out now and surrender!'

But the people did not answer.

Hezekiah sent men to tell the prophet Isaiah and ask his help. The prophet heard them out.

'Tell Hezekiah not to be afraid,' Isaiah answered. 'God *can* save the city—and he will.'

King Sennacherib of Assyria wrote a letter to King Hezekiah.

'I will destroy your city,' he said. 'Your God will not be able to save you.'

Hezekiah took the letter into the Temple and talked to God about it.

'You are the only God,' he said. 'You made the world. You are King above every king. Please rescue us from the Assyrians.'

Once again Isaiah sent the king a message.

'God has heard the insults of the king of Assyria. "I gave him power," God says. "But now I will take him captive. He will not enter this city. His soldiers will not shoot one arrow against it. I will defend and protect Jerusalem."'

That night a terrible thing happened in the Assyrian camp. Thousands and thousands of Assyrian soldiers died. No one knew why. Next morning the camp was full of dead bodies.

And the king of Assyria heard rumours of an invasion. He went home to his capital city of Nineveh. And not long after, he was murdered by two of his sons.

Jerusalem was left in peace.

Isaiah sees into the future
When Hezekiah was old, men came to him from the
king of Babylonia. Hezekiah treated them as friends and
proudly showed them all his treasures.

Then Isaiah said to the king:

'The Babylonians are our friends now. But God
says that one day all your treasures, and many of your
people, will be carried captive to Babylon.'

For God had shared with Isaiah some of the things
that were going to happen to his people.

'God saved Jerusalem from the Assyrians,' Isaiah
told the people. 'But unless you really trust him and
obey his laws, one day Jerusalem will fall. Enemy
soldiers will take you to live in exile in a far-off land.
But God will never give you up. He will bring you
home again.'

The prophet's eyes shone.

He knew some of the wonderful things God had
planned. They would not happen now. Not even soon.
But in the future. One day, God would send his own
King.

'God will send us a child, who will be our ruler.
He will be called, "Wonderful Counsellor,"
"Mighty God," "Eternal Father,"
"Prince of Peace." . . .
He will rule as King David's successor.'

'We must make way for God's King,' Isaiah said.

'Clear a road for him through the desert.
Fill in the valleys.
Level the mountains.
So that people everywhere can see God's glory.'

All that Isaiah said came true. But not then.
Many years later.

Josiah's discovery

The kings who succeeded Hezekiah spoiled all the good that he had done. Once again the people made images and worshipped them. They even killed their own children and offered them to these 'gods'. They turned to witchcraft and worshipped the sun and stars.

The people of Judah were following the bad example of Israel. Soon Judah, too, would be destroyed. But there was one last king—Josiah—who was loyal to God.

Josiah was only a boy—like Joash—when he became king. When he was eighteen he gave orders that God's Temple must be repaired. Workmen found an old and important-looking book hidden in one of the store rooms. Hilkiah the priest gave it to Josiah's secretary, and he read it out loud to the king. Josiah listened in growing dismay.

'This is the book of God's laws,' he said. 'And it is years and years since these laws were kept. We have broken our promise to God. We must find out what he wants us to do.'

'Let's ask Huldah about it,' Hilkiah said.

Huldah was God's prophetess, and she was famous for her wisdom. They hurried to her house in the city.

'What does it mean? What are we to do?' they asked.

'This is what God says,' Huldah answered. 'My people have not obeyed me. They have worshipped images. And they will be punished. But because the king is loyal to me, I will not punish them in his lifetime.'

King Josiah sent for the leaders and all the people. They gathered outside the Temple, and he read the book of the law out loud to them. Everyone promised to obey God's commands.

Then Josiah began a great 'clean-up' campaign, to get rid of all the images of Baal and the other gods his people had worshipped.

He burned all the wooden images.

He tore down all the altars to gods and demons.

He destroyed the place in the Valley of Hinnom where people had given their children as a burnt-offering to the god Molech.

He burnt the chariots they used in worshipping the sun.

Throughout the kingdom, all the pagan places of worship set up by earlier kings of Judah were destroyed.

The priests of Baal, the wizards and the witches were driven out.

'Now we can celebrate the Passover Festival,' Josiah said, 'as God's people did when they came out of Egypt.'

No Passover like this one had been held in the kingdom for hundreds of years. Thousands of sheep and lambs, goats and bulls were killed and roasted. Each family group ate the feast together.

The festival lasted for seven days. And the people worshipped God.

King Josiah loved God with all his heart. There was no king like him in Judah, before or after. But, sadly, when Josiah was killed in battle, the people slipped back to their old ways. All that the king had done only delayed God's punishment.

Jeremiah and the fall of Jerusalem

Josiah was still king of Judah when God called Jeremiah to be his prophet. Jeremiah was young and shy—not at all the sort of person to enjoy standing up and making public speeches.

'I chose you to be my prophet before you were born,' God said. 'Don't be afraid. I know you better than you know yourself. I will tell you what to say. And I will keep you safe.'

Jeremiah really had no choice. God's message was like fire—so hot that it seemed to burn him if he kept it to himself. He simply *had* to speak.

He was living in difficult times. The little kingdom of Judah was in the middle of a tug-of-war as the great nations to the north and south fought for even greater power. King Josiah died in battle, trying to stop the king of Egypt from marching north, through his land, to help the Assyrians fight off the Babylonians.

Four years later, Nebuchadnezzar of Babylon won a

great battle. He defeated Egypt, and took control of Judah.

All this time Jeremiah was faithfully telling his people what God had to say, warning them of the terrible things that would happen if they did not turn back to God.

But it seemed to make no difference. The people went on worshipping images just as before. No one took Jeremiah seriously. They thought he was a joke, a bit funny in the head, with all his talk of doom. The people were deaf to God's word, and blind to see what was coming.

Jeremiah tried using pictures to get his point across. He went to the potter's house and watched him at work. As the wheel spun round, the potter shaped the clay into a pot or a jug. Sometimes it went wrong. Then he squashed the lump of clay and started all over again.

God said to Jeremiah,

'The people of Israel are in my hands, just like the clay in the potter's hands. I have the right to destroy and remake them—and I will, if they do not listen. They must change their ways and stop doing what they know is wrong.'

Jeremiah told the people—but still they would not listen.

Another day, Jeremiah stood in front of the Temple.

'This is what God says: If you will not listen to me and obey my laws, I will destroy the Temple and the city of Jerusalem.'

It was too much for the priests. They refused to let Jeremiah come near the Temple after that. He was arrested and beaten.

But no one can keep God quiet! Jeremiah was no longer free to speak God's message—but he could still write it. He filled a long roll of parchment (there were no books or writing-pads in those days) with all he had to say. It was read to the king—and the king was so angry he threw the roll of parchment on the fire.

But even that was useless. Jeremiah simply wrote it all out again!

'God's word is like fire,' Jeremiah said. 'You will never be able to put it out. It is like a hammer that can break the hardest rock into tiny pieces.'

The king of Judah refused to pay his taxes to King Nebuchadnezzar. He plotted rebellion. And he lost his throne!

Nebuchadnezzar's army came to Jerusalem and took him away to Babylon, with thousands of other captives (among them a young man called Ezekiel*).

Zedekiah was made king—the last king of Judah. But still God's people had not learnt their lesson.

'God says, give in to the Babylonians,' Jeremiah declared, 'or they will destroy you. Give up worshipping useless images. Return to the living God before it is too late. Time is short.'

Jeremiah was the most unpopular man in Jerusalem.

'Traitor! Traitor!' the people shouted. 'You are in the pay of the enemy.'

And they seized the prophet and beat him and threw him into prison.

*See page 138. Daniel had been taken hostage a few years earlier.

When Zedekiah had been king for ten years, he too rebelled. Nebuchadnezzar came back and besieged Jerusalem.

'Surrender, if you want to save your lives,' Jeremiah said to the people. 'God will give this city to the Babylonians.'

The leaders were furious. They flung Jeremiah into a deep well. There was no water in it, only mud. And they left him to starve to death. But Ebedmelech—a man from Ethiopia, who worked at the palace—went to the king and asked him to save the prophet's life. Then he and three other men let down ropes, and Jeremiah was pulled to safety.

King Zedekiah had secret talks with the prophet.

'What am I to do?' he asked.

'Surrender—the city will be destroyed,' Jeremiah answered.

But instead of doing as Jeremiah said, the king tried to escape, and save his own life.

The Babylonians caught him. They killed his two sons, and blinded him.

They broke through the city wall, smashed the palace and God's Temple and the houses, and set them on fire. They carried away the Temple treasure.

And they took the people back with them to work as slaves in far-off Babylonia—the same land from which God had called Abraham hundreds of years before.

Jeremiah stayed behind with the few who were left. All his warnings had been ignored. God had punished his disobedient people. But he had not stopped loving them.

Jeremiah wrote a comforting letter to the exiles:

'God says: I give you my promise that one day I will bring you back home. You will learn to love me in the land of exile. You will remember my laws and begin to do what you know is right. Look forward to the day when I will bring you back from exile to your own land.'

Ezekiel and the exiles

Ezekiel was feeling very homesick. All his life he had looked forward to his thirtieth birthday, when he would serve in the Temple as one of God's priests.

And here he was, hundreds of miles from his homeland. Ezekiel was one of ten thousand captives taken from the hills and valleys of Judah to work on the plains of Babylonia, when King Nebuchadnezzar first took control of Judah.

Five years had passed since Ezekiel left home.

'How far away the Temple is,' Ezekiel thought. 'How far away God seems.'

A sudden gust of wind made him look up. Was that a storm coming? A strange dark cloud raced towards him. Lightning flashed. It was so close now that Ezekiel could see into the centre of the storm. There were four creatures like the winged beasts that guarded the box of God's law in the Temple—flying wing to wing—and wheels that could turn every way; and eyes that could see in all directions.

Above the darkness, Ezekiel could see a dazzling blue—far brighter than the sky—shot with all the colours of the rainbow.

Then he heard a voice, a voice that shook the earth. Ezekiel trembled. Could it be God himself, here in the land of Babylon?

'Mortal man,' said the voice, 'I am sending you to warn my people in exile. They have rebelled and turned against me. Tell them to mend their ways. I will give you the words to speak.'

Then the vision was gone. Ezekiel walked trembling back to the camp. God was here—he was everywhere—after all. And he had given him a special job to do—not in the Temple, but in the camp, among the exiles.

God gave Ezekiel many visions after that—terrible
and wonderful visions. He showed Ezekiel how
Nebuchadnezzar would march into Judah again,
conquer Jerusalem and destroy the Temple.

Ezekiel told the others about it—and not just in
words. He acted the scene so vividly that no one could
forget it.

'This is our own fault,' he said. 'After all God's
love and goodness to us we broke his laws, we did
wrong, we even worshipped useless images. This is our
punishment.'

News came at last that Nebuchadnezzar had
captured Jerusalem and destroyed the city and Temple,
just as Ezekiel had said he would. The exiles were in
despair.

'We have no future now,' they said. 'There is no
hope. God has given us up.'

Ezekiel did his best to comfort them.

'It's not true,' he said. 'God still loves us.'

But the people would not be comforted.

So God gave Ezekiel a special new vision. He was
standing in a valley, and on the ground all around him
there were bones—the dry bones of old skeletons.

'Tell these bones that I will make them into living,
breathing people,' God said.

Ezekiel did as he was told. And as he spoke God's
words, a miracle happened. Bone joined to bone. The
skeletons stood up. They became flesh-and-blood
bodies! And God breathed life into them through his
words.

'Tell my people what I can do,' God said to Ezekiel.
'I will breathe new life into them and make them one
nation again. I will take them home to their own land.
And this time they will be loyal to me. Tell them it's a
promise. They should know that I always keep my
promises.'

The story of Daniel

Daniel was only a boy when King Nebuchadnezzar carried him off from his home in Jerusalem to Babylon as a hostage.

Soon after they arrived, Daniel and his three friends were chosen for special training. They were all good-looking boys, from some of the best families of Judah. And they had brains!

'Put them in my school for three years,' said the king. 'Teach them our language. Let them study our writings; let them learn from our great thinkers. I will supply the best food and wine. I want them to be fit, as well as clever.'

Now God had given his people special rules about what they could and could not eat. And Daniel and his friends wanted to keep God's laws. So they asked the guard who was in charge of them to let them eat vegetables and drink water, instead of the food the king supplied.

'It's more than my life's worth to let you get thin or fall ill,' said the guard. 'But you can try it for ten days, and then we'll see.'

After ten days, Daniel and his friends were fitter and stronger than the young men who had been eating the royal food. And they did well in class, too. So the guard let them go on with their diet.

And at the end of three years they won all the prizes. They knew even more than the wise men of Babylon. So the king made them members of his court.

The dream

One night, the king had a terrifying dream. He woke in a panic and sent for his wise men.

'I can't remember what the dream was,' he said. 'You'll have to tell me. And then you must say what it means.'

The wise men were very worried when they heard this. They were good at meanings—but they had to know the dream first.

'If you will only tell us your dream, we will explain it,' they said. The king flew into a great rage.

'I'll have you torn limb from limb,' he shouted.

'But no one could do what you ask,' the men said.

Then the king ordered his soldiers to execute all the wise men in Babylon.

They came to arrest Daniel.

'Let me speak to the king,' he said. 'I will tell him the dream and what it means.'

Daniel told his friends, and they all prayed to God, asking him to explain the mystery. And God revealed

the dream and its meaning to Daniel.

The king began to respect Daniel's God.

'Your God is a God of gods if he can reveal mysteries like this,' he said.

The golden statue

But a few years later, King Nebuchadnezzar made a great gold statue of one of his gods. It was ninety feet high. All the important people went to the dedication of the statue—governors, councillors, magistrates. The best musicians were there, with pipes and lyres and harps.

'As soon as the music starts, everyone is to bow down and worship the god,' said the king, 'or I'll have him burnt to death in the hottest furnace.'

They all did as they were told—all, that is, except Daniel's three friends. (Daniel himself had remained at the royal court.) They spoke bravely to the king.

'Our God is able to save us from the fire. Nothing is too hard for him. But even if he doesn't, we will not worship any other god. We will not bow down to the statue.'

The king was in such a fury that he had the furnace made seven times hotter than usual. The men were bound hand and foot and thrown in.

Then the king rubbed his eyes in amazement. He could see *four* men, not three, walking calmly through the flames! '—and the fourth one,' he said, 'looks like a god!'

'Come out!' he called—and the three friends came! They were no longer tied up. But the flames had not touched their clothes, or burnt a hair of their heads! They did not even smell of smoke.

'The God who can do this is indeed a great God,' said the king. 'Let no one say a word against the God of these men!'

Belshazzar's feast

The years passed. Nebuchadnezzar died, and Belshazzar became king of Babylon. He gave a great feast for a thousand of his lords. And he drank more wine than was good for him. He wanted to show off his riches.

'Bring me the gold and silver cups and bowls that Nebuchadnezzar brought from the Temple in Jerusalem,' he shouted. And his servants ran to obey.

Then the king and all his lords drank to their own

gods—images made of metal, wood and stone—from the cups which belonged to God's Temple.

They were all shouting and laughing and making a great noise when they saw a human hand appear out of thin air. Just a hand. It began to write on the plaster wall. The guests fell silent, and the king went white as a ghost.

'Call my wise men,' he croaked. 'The man who can tell me what this means shall be made Prime Minister.' But none of the wise men knew what the writing meant.

Then the queen mother remembered how Daniel had told King Nebuchadnezzar his dream. So they sent for Daniel.

'Tell me what this means and I will make you rich and powerful,' said the king.

'Keep your gifts,' answered Daniel. 'What I have to say won't please you. You have dishonoured God by drinking to your gods from the cups which belong to his Temple. God says the days of your kingdom are numbered. It will be given to the Medes and Persians.'

That same night Belshazzar was killed. The Medes and Persians captured Babylon, and placed their own leader, Darius, on the throne.

The plot to kill Daniel

Darius made Daniel one of his three chief rulers. Daniel was by now a very old man. But he served the king honestly and loyally. And he still prayed to God, as he had always done, regular as clockwork three times a day, kneeling at his open window, facing towards far-off Jerusalem.

The other leaders were jealous of Daniel, and plotted against him. What could they accuse him of? He never put a foot wrong. It would have to be something to do with his religion.

So they persuaded the king to make a new law—one

that could not be changed.

'For thirty days no one must ask for anything from any god. Whoever breaks this law will be thrown to the lions.'

Daniel knew that the king had signed the order. But he still prayed to God, openly, three times a day.

Daniel's enemies were delighted. Their plot had worked. They hurried to tell the king.

Darius was angry and upset. He thought very hard, but he could find no way to save Daniel.

That night Daniel was thrown into a deep pit full of hungry lions.

The king couldn't eat his supper. He sent all the royal musicians and entertainers away. He did not sleep a wink. As soon as it began to grow light he hurried to the lion-pit.

'Daniel,' he called out. 'Was your God able to save you from the lions?' He did not expect a reply.

But to his amazement Daniel's voice answered,

'Yes, your majesty. The lions have not hurt me. God knew that I was innocent. I have done you no wrong.'

'Set him free at once,' Darius cried. 'And throw the men who accused him to the lions!'

So Daniel came out unhurt, because of his trust in God.

King Darius made a new law.

'Let everyone in my kingdom tremble and fear before the God of Daniel, who saved him from the lions. He is the living God, for ever and ever.'

Back home to Jerusalem!

Cyrus, the Persian king who now reigned in Babylon, was a good man. He made a proclamation.

'God has told me to let his people, the Jews,* go home and rebuild his Temple in Jerusalem. They are all free to go. And I will return all the treasures King Nebuchadnezzar took from the Temple before he destroyed it.'

The streets of Babylon rang with shouts of joy that day!

'The exile is over. God has kept his promise. We can go home!'

God's people were longing to worship him in their own land again. The years of exile had brought them to their senses, and taught them to love God and obey him.

Forty-two thousand people set out across the desert, with their servants and all that they owned. Their horses and mules and camels were piled high with goods, and with food for the journey.

When they reached Jerusalem at last, their first thought was to start work on God's Temple. Gifts of gold and silver poured in for the building fund. Eagerly they laid the foundations of the Temple. The people who had been living in the land while the Jews were in exile offered to help.

'We worship God too,' they said.

But the Jews wanted to do it all on their own.

Then the people of the land made trouble. The

*They were given this name because they came from Judah.

work was held up for a long time. God's prophets spoke
out.

'You should be ashamed,' they said. 'You are busy
with your own houses while God's Temple lies in
ruins.'

Then the Jews began work again. The Temple was
finished at last. It was not as splendid as King
Solomon's Temple. But it was a fine building, all the
same.

Ezra, the scholar

The years passed. Back in Babylon, Ezra, a scholar who studied God's law, was worried. The Jews in Israel did not seem to know God's law. He asked the king if he could go and teach them. The king had a great respect for Ezra.

'You may go,' he said, 'and take any others who want to go with you. I will give you silver and gold for God's Temple and anything else you need.'

'God has put this into the king's heart,' Ezra thought. 'The journey is dangerous. There may be robbers on the road. But God is able to keep us safe. I won't ask the king for guards.'

And God did keep them safe.

In Jerusalem Ezra found many things wrong. The men had married foreign wives who brought their own gods with them. This was just what had caused the trouble before the exile.

'You have broken your promises to God,' Ezra said. 'These things must be put right.' So Ezra taught the people to obey God's laws.

Governor Nehemiah

The Temple had been rebuilt, but the city was still in ruins. The walls were broken and burnt.

When the news reached Nehemiah, back at the royal palace in Persia, he wept.

Nehemiah was an important man at court—in charge of the king of Persia's wine. He was a Jew, a man who loved God and who cared very much for his own people. For days he went without food and prayed to God. His face was sad—and the king soon noticed.

'What is the matter?' he asked.

'Your majesty, Jerusalem is in ruins,' Nehemiah answered—and he sent a quick prayer to God that the king would help him. 'Please let me go back and rebuild it.'

God answered Nehemiah's prayer. The king not only let him go, he ordered the governors of his provinces to see that Nehemiah got through safely, and to give him any help he needed.

So Nehemiah arrived in Jerusalem.

He waited till it was dark. Then he rode all round the city, inspecting the walls.

Next day he spoke to the priests and leaders and all the people.

'These broken-down walls are a disgrace,' he said. 'Let's start rebuilding! God will help us.' And he told them how God had answered his prayer, and the Persian king had let him come.

Nehemiah knew how to pray—and he knew how to work. He was appointed governor of Judah, and he soon had everyone organized. Each family worked on the section of wall nearest to their home. So they wanted to get on and make a really good job of it.

But the people of the land were afraid. They did not want Jerusalem to be a strong walled city again. The work must be stopped.

At first they made fun of the Jewish workers.

'What kind of wall do you think you can build?' they taunted. 'Even a fox could knock it down.'

But the Jewish people were eager to work, and they simply carried on building. The walls began to grow.

Then their enemies planned an attack. Nehemiah prayed for God's help—and set a guard. While half the

people worked, the others stood by with weapons ready.

The enemy tried new tricks.

'We want to talk,' they said.

'This is important work. No time to stop and talk,' Nehemiah answered.

Then they threatened to tell the king that Nehemiah was plotting rebellion. But they could not frighten him.

With God's help, the work was finished. It had taken fifty-two days. Jerusalem was a strong walled city once again—a city to be proud of.

The Jews held a great celebration. They marched all round the city on top of the wall, shouting and singing their thanks to God. The priests blew their trumpets. The bands played. Everyone was happy.

Ezra the scholar read God's law out loud to the people and explained what it meant. The people asked God to forgive all the wrong they had done. They promised always to love God and keep his law.

So governor Nehemiah and Ezra the scholar led God's people and taught them what was right.

The plot that failed

King Xerxes of Persia gave a great banquet for all the men in his capital city of Susa. It was held in the palace gardens, and it lasted seven days. The wine was served in solid gold cups, and drinks were on the house—as much as anyone wanted.

Inside the palace, Queen Vashti was holding a banquet for the women.

On the seventh day, when he was feeling rather merry, the king decided to show off his beautiful queen.

'Bring Queen Vashti here,' he ordered his servants.

But the queen refused to come!

She made the king look silly in front of all his guests. He was furious.

King Xerxes sent for his advisers.

'If the other women hear about this,' they said, 'every wife in Persia will think she can disobey her husband.'

There was only one thing to do.

'Send Queen Vashti away,' commanded the king. 'I will have a new queen.'

So the search for a new queen began.

All the most beautiful girls in Persia were sent to the palace. For a year they stayed in the king's harem. They were put on a special diet, and every day they were massaged with sweet-scented oils.

Then the king sent for each of them in turn.

The most beautiful of them all was Esther, the adopted daughter of Mordecai the Jew. Everyone loved her. And as soon as the king saw her, he chose her to be his queen.

One day Mordecai heard about a plot to kill the king. He told Esther. And the king was very grateful. He wrote Mordecai's name in the official palace records.

Some time after this a man called Haman was made chief of staff to the king. He was proud and vain and cruel. Everyone had to kneel before him. Only Mordecai refused.

'I am a Jew,' he said. 'And my people kneel only to God.'

From that moment, Haman made up his mind to kill Mordecai and all the Jews. He went to the king.

'There is a nation in your kingdom that refuses to obey your laws. Let me have them destroyed.'

The king gave Haman the ring he used as a royal seal. And Haman sent orders sealed with the king's seal to the governors of all the provinces, telling them to kill the Jews on a certain day.

No one at the palace knew that Esther was a Jewish girl.

Mordecai and all the Jews went into mourning. They ate no food, and they wept out loud.

'Whatever is it?' Esther asked. And Mordecai told her.

'Go to the king and plead for the lives of your people,' he said.

'It's a month since the king sent for me,' Esther replied. 'And if I go to him without being asked, he may have me killed.'

'But God may have made you queen in order to save us all,' said Mordecai. 'No one else can speak to the king for us.'

So Esther went to the king. Haman was with him—but he was glad to see her. Esther waited till the moment was right. She invited them both to dinner that night and it went well.

'Come back again tomorrow,' she said.

Haman was flattered. Dinner alone with the king and queen! But the thought of Mordecai spoilt everything. So he ordered his men to build a gallows, ready to hang the Jew next day.

But that night the king could not sleep. He sat up, reading through the palace records—and there was Mordecai's name.

'I must reward him,' he thought.

So instead of being hanged, as Haman had planned, Mordecai was given royal honours.

The next night, at dinner, the king thought how lovely his queen was looking.

'I will give you anything you want,' he said to her. 'You have only to ask.'

'I and all my people are to be killed,' Esther answered. 'I ask for my life and the lives of my people.'

The king turned pale.

'Who is responsible for this?'

'Haman,' she answered.

'He has had a gallows made, ready to hang Mordecai,' one of the servants added.

'Then hang him on his own gallows,' said the king. And that was what they did.

Esther saved the lives of all her people that night. And the king made Mordecai his new chief of staff.

The runaway

Generally speaking, the prophets (the messengers God sent to his people) did as God said. But there was one exception: Jonah.

God spoke to Jonah.

'Go to Nineveh,' he said, 'and tell the people I know all about their wickedness. In forty days Nineveh shall be destroyed.'

Now Nineveh was the capital of Assyria. And the Assyrians were the enemies of God's people. So Jonah did not mind telling the people of Nineveh that God was about to destroy them!

'But God is loving,' he thought. 'He forgives people and lets them have a second chance. He won't destroy Nineveh. And I shall look silly.'

So Jonah set off—not for Nineveh, but for the port of Jaffa, where he caught a boat that was bound for Spain.

As soon as the ship was out at sea, God sent a great storm. The captain and crew were terrified.

'Pray to your gods,' they cried to the passengers.
'Pray for your lives.'

Jonah was fast asleep. The captain shook him hard.

'Pray, like everyone else,' he said.

'I can't ask God for help', Jonah said. 'I've been
running away from him. It's God who has sent this
storm. Throw me overboard. Then the sea will be
calm.'

At first the captain refused. But the storm got
worse and worse. In the end he did as Jonah said.

As Jonah plunged down, down into the water, the
sea grew calm. And on board ship the men gave thanks
to Jonah's God.

Jonah thought he would drown. As the waves
closed over his head he called out to God for help. And
God sent a huge fish, that swallowed him alive.

Alone in the dark, inside the fish for three days, Jonah was sorry he had disobeyed God. And he said so.

Then God gave the word and the fish threw Jonah up on to a beach. He had never been so glad to see the sun!

He went straight to Nineveh to tell the people God's message.

'In forty days Nineveh will be destroyed!'

And the people took God at his word. They changed their ways—every one of them, from the lowest slave to the king in his palace. God was glad. Because they gave up their wicked ways, he did not destroy them.

Jonah sat down outside the city, feeling angry and miserable.

'Didn't I say this was what you'd do?' he said to God. 'That was why I tried to run away. I knew how kind you are. So now, just let me die!'

But God didn't let Jonah die. Instead he made a plant grow up and shade him from the burning sun.

Jonah felt better.

Next day the plant died and the sun beat down on him.

'I was glad of that plant,' Jonah said. 'I'm sorry it's gone.'

'Now you're beginning to learn,' God said. 'You're sorry for a plant that you did nothing for. You didn't make it grow. So don't you think I have a right to be sorry for all those people in Nineveh, and innocent children? Not to mention the animals. I gave them life and I go to a lot of trouble taking care of them.'

And Jonah began, at last, to understand.

The story of Jesus and his followers

THE NEW TESTAMENT

After God's people returned from exile,
hundreds of years went by. Then the Romans
marched in and took control of the country.
There were Roman soldiers everywhere.
The people had to pay tax to Rome.
They hated it and longed for freedom.
The prophets had promised that one day God
would send his own King, the 'Messiah'.
'He will drive out the Romans and set us free,'
the people thought.
But this was not what the prophets meant.
So when God's King did come,
most people did not recognize him.
It began like this . . .

A girl named Mary

In the town of Nazareth in the north of Israel (the district called Galilee) there lived a girl named Mary. She was just an ordinary girl. She helped her mother bake the bread and spin the wool and fetch the water like the other girls. When she was old enough her parents arranged for her to marry Joseph, the town carpenter. But then, one day, something quite extraordinary happened.

Mary was busy with the day's jobs as usual, her mind full of the coming wedding, when she looked up and saw a stranger standing watching her. Before she could say a word, the man spoke:

'I am Gabriel, one of God's messenger-angels,' he said. 'I have a message for you from God.'

Mary could hardly believe her ears. She felt scared, and she wondered what the angel could mean.

'Don't be frightened,' the angel went on. 'God knows all about you and he loves you. He has sent me to tell you that he's chosen you for a very special honour. You are to be the mother of God's promised King. The baby will be God's own Son.'

'But I don't understand,' Mary said. 'I'm not even married yet . . .' Her head was buzzing with questions.

'This is something God will do. Nothing is too hard for him. You remember your cousin Elizabeth? Everyone thought she could never have children. But now she is expecting a baby. You see, there is nothing God cannot do.'

When Mary heard this, she knew that she could trust God to do whatever he said. She did not have to understand it all.

'I will do whatever God wants,' she said.

'His name is John'

As soon as she could, Mary set out to visit her cousin Elizabeth. It was a long journey, but at last she arrived at the house where Elizabeth lived with her husband Zechariah.

'As soon as I heard the news, I had to come,' Mary said. And she began to tell Elizabeth all that had happened. But to her surprise, Elizabeth already knew.

'It's a wonderful thing,' Elizabeth said, 'that God has chosen you to be the mother of the King.'

And she began to tell Mary her own surprising story . . .

Elizabeth and Zechariah had longed for a baby. They had asked God about it in their prayers. But the years passed and no baby came. They began to grow old, and they gave up hope.

Zechariah was a priest, and his turn came to go to the Temple at Jerusalem and take part in the daily service. He was specially chosen to go inside the Temple and burn the sweet-smelling incense on the altar.

While he was there, alone, God's messenger-angel, Gabriel, came to him.

'Don't be afraid, Zechariah,' the angel said. 'God has sent me to tell you that he has heard your prayers for a baby. You and Elizabeth will have a son. You are to call him John. He will grow up to be a great man and make you very happy. God has chosen your son to tell his people that their King is coming. John will help them get ready to welcome him.'

But Zechariah really couldn't believe it. He and Elizabeth were too old to have a baby!

'Because you have not believed God's word,' the angel said, 'you won't be able to speak, from this moment until the day God's promise comes true.'

When Zechariah finished his duties in the Temple he went home. He couldn't speak a word. Elizabeth couldn't think what had happened to him. She was very worried. Then Zechariah wrote it all down, to explain . . .

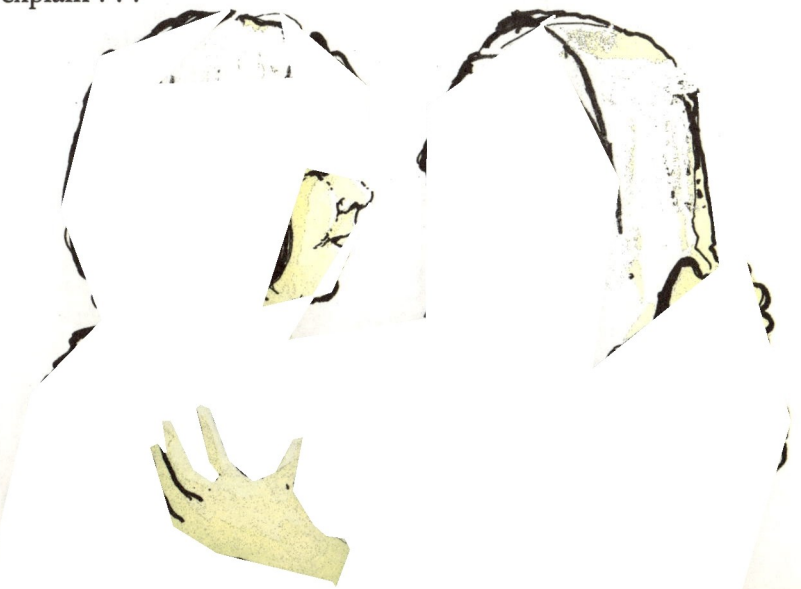

'God has kept his prom... ...old Mary. 'The baby is due to be born in four months' time. But Zechariah still can't speak.'

Mary stayed with Elizabeth and Zechariah for three months. Elizabeth's baby was almost due when Mary went home to Nazareth.

Elizabeth's baby arrived. It was a boy. All the family and friends were so pleased for her! They began to discuss the baby's name. Everyone wanted to call him Zechariah, after his father. But Elizabeth said, No, the baby's name was John.

'But no one is called John in our family!' they argued. And they turned to Zechariah, to ask what he wanted the baby to be called.

Zechariah picked up his writing-tablet. Then, to their surprise, he wrote:

'His name is John.'

And at that moment Zechariah's voice came back. He was able to speak again. And the first thing he did was to thank God, out loud, for his little son.

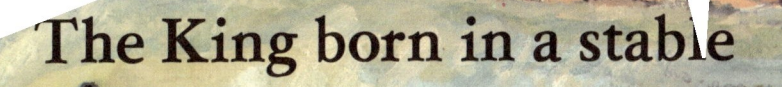

The King born in a stable

Joseph the carpenter was worried. Mary, the girl he loved, was expecting a baby. It wasn't his baby; and they weren't married. The gossip had started already. He would have to break off the engagement.

But that night he had a dream. And in the dream God's messenger-angel spoke to him:

'Don't break off your engagement to Mary,' the angel said. 'She has done nothing wrong. God has chosen her to be the mother of his Son—the promised King. You are to call the baby Jesus (the Saviour), because he is going to save his people from their sins.'

When Joseph woke up, it was as if a great weight had been lifted from his mind. It didn't matter what anyone said! He would marry Mary and take care of her and the baby.

Not long after this the Roman Emperor, Augustus, issued an order. Everyone in the Roman Empire must register at the town his family came from. Augustus wanted to make sure he had everyone on his list, and that they paid their taxes!

Joseph's family was descended from King David. So he had to go to Bethlehem, where King David was born. He had to take Mary on the long journey south through the hills—eighty miles of rough dirt roads. The donkey carried their food, warm cloaks for the chilly nights, and clothes for the baby who was due to be born any day.

Mary was very tired when they arrived at last. And there was nowhere for them to stay. The inn was already crowded with travellers. The inn-keeper felt sorry for Mary—but the only space he had left was the stable. It was dirty and smelly in there with the animals. But at least Mary could rest—and there was nowhere else.

That night Mary's baby son was born. She wrapped him up warmly in the clothes she had made, and put him in a manger to sleep.

On the hills around the town, shepherds kept watch, looking after their flocks. The night was dark and everything was quiet—just a little bleat now and then from one of the sheep.

Then suddenly there was a blaze of light—so bright, the men had to shield their eyes. And out of the brightness came the voice of God's messenger-angel.

'Don't be afraid. I've come with good news—for you and all the world. The Saviour has come—God's promised King—born today in Bethlehem. You will find the baby asleep in a manger.'

Then the shepherds saw a great crowd of angels, all singing praises to God.

'Glory to God in heaven,' they sang, 'and peace to all who love him on earth.'

When the angels had gone and the sky was dark again, the shepherds began to talk among themselves.

'We must go to Bethlehem,' they said, 'and see what has happened.'

They made sure the sheep were safe. Then they hurried into the town. They found Mary and Joseph in the stable at the inn—and a new-born baby lying in the manger. Then they knew that what the angels had told them was true.

They told Mary and Joseph all that had happened. Then they went back to the sheep, telling everyone they met on the way about the baby and the angel's message. They sang as they walked along, thanking God for all they had seen. It was a night they would never forget.

Strangers—and a star

When Mary's baby was eight days old, he was given his name—Jesus. Soon it was time for Joseph and Mary to do as the Jewish law said, and dedicate their first son to God. So they took the baby to God's Temple at Jerusalem.

There was a good old man called Simeon living in the city. God had promised him that before he died he would see the King. Simeon was there when Mary and Joseph came to the Temple with Jesus. He took the baby in his arms and thanked God for him.

'God has kept his promise,' Simeon said. 'Now I shall die content. For I have seen the Saviour.'

Anna, too, saw the baby and gave thanks to God. She was an old lady of eighty-four who spent all her time in the Temple, saying prayers to God and thanking him. Anna told everyone in the city that the King they were waiting for had come.

Mary and Joseph were amazed at all that had happened. They went back to Bethlehem. And not long after, there was another surprise.

Strangers from the east—men who studied the stars—arrived in Jerusalem.

'Tell us where we can find the baby who is born to be King of the Jews,' they said. 'We have seen his star and come to pay him homage.'

Soon the whole town was talking about the wise men and their strange question. What could it mean?

The Romans had made a man called Herod king of the Jews. He was most alarmed when he heard the news. Herod did not want a rival king in his land. He

sent for the priests and teachers of God's law.

'When the Saviour comes, where will he be born?' Herod asked.

'In Bethlehem,' they answered. 'That is what God's prophets say.'

Then King Herod had a secret meeting with the strangers, to find out when they first saw the star.

'Go and look for the child in Bethlehem,' he said. 'And when you find him, let me know, so that I can come and pay him homage too.'

So the strangers came to Bethlehem, still following the star. They found the baby in one of the houses, with Mary his mother. Then they opened their bags and brought out presents—strange, rich presents to give to a baby!—gold, sweet-smelling frankincense and a spicy ointment called myrrh.

God warned them in a dream not to go back to King Herod. So they went home by another road.

After they had gone, an angel came to Joseph in a dream.

'Get up, quickly,' he said. 'You must take Mary and the baby to Egypt. Go at once. It is not safe for you

here. King Herod will be looking for Jesus. He wants to kill him. Stay in Egypt until I tell you it is safe to leave.'

Joseph lost no time. He woke Mary, and they quickly packed a few clothes, the things they needed for the baby, and Joseph's tools. It was still dark when they set off down the dusty road south through the desert to Egypt, where another Joseph had saved the lives of his family long, long before.

Herod was furious when he realized how the wise men had tricked him. He was a cruel man who had many enemies. And he was always afraid that someone would murder him and seize the throne. He intended to make quite sure this baby king did not grow up. So he sent his soldiers to Bethlehem. They had orders to kill every boy under two years old. King Herod was taking no chances.

No one in Bethlehem could ever forget that terrible day—and the people hated Herod more than ever.

Not very long after this, King Herod died. The angel came to Joseph again, in a dream, and told him it was safe to go home. So Joseph and Mary and Jesus went home to Nazareth.

Mary never forgot Simeon and Anna, the shepherds and the wise men. She often thought about the wonderful things that happened when Jesus was born.

As the years passed, Jesus grew up. He was strong, and quick to learn. God loved him and so did everyone who knew him.

The boy in the Temple

Every year, in the Spring, Joseph and Mary went to Jerusalem for the annual Passover Festival. (At Passover time each family killed a lamb and ate a special meal, to remind them of how God had rescued his people from slavery in Egypt.) When he was twelve, Jesus went with them, joining the happy groups of visitors who crowded into the city.

The busy, exciting days of the feast were soon over, and it was time to go home. Mary and Joseph set off with the crowd returning to Nazareth.

The boys were always running ahead or lagging behind, so Mary and Joseph did not notice Jesus was missing until the evening. None of their friends had seen him.

Mary and Joseph were much too worried to sleep that night. Next morning they went back to Jerusalem, looking for Jesus. Another whole day passed before at last they found him—in the Temple, listening to the men who taught God's laws, and asking questions. Everyone who heard him was amazed at how much he understood.

'Why did you do this to us?' Mary asked. 'Your father and I have been so worried.'

Jesus seemed almost surprised at her question.

'But surely you knew I had to be here, in my Father's house,' he said.

Mary and Joseph were puzzled by Jesus' answer. They were forgetting that Jesus was no ordinary boy, that God was his Father.

So they returned to Nazareth, where Jesus was as obedient to them as he had always been before.

The King's herald

Zechariah helped his little son to learn and understand
the scriptures—God's laws and the words of the
prophets. From the start, John was trained for the work
God had chosen him to do.

When he was older, he lived alone in the desert. He
wore clothes made of rough camels' hair, with a leather
belt round his waist. He lived on locusts and wild
honey.

There in the desert God gave John his message. And when he was grown up he began to preach and teach. Crowds flocked to hear this strange, wild-looking man who spoke with such power.

'God's King is coming soon,' he said. 'Make sure you are ready. Change your ways, and God will forgive you.'

John was very outspoken. He told people what they were doing wrong. Many of those who heard him really wanted to live better lives. So he took them down into the River Jordan, 'baptizing' them in the water as a sign that their past sins were washed away. They could make a fresh clean start. When they asked him what they ought to do, John answered:

'Share your food with those who are hungry. If you have more clothes than you need, share them too.' He told the tax collectors to stop cheating and the soldiers to be content with their pay.

People began to wonder if John could be God's promised King. But he said, No.

'I am only the King's herald,' he said, '—someone sent to tell you he is coming. The King is much greater than I am.'

Jesus travelled south from Nazareth to see John. Although they were related, they had not met before. But John knew at once that Jesus was God's promised King.

'Why have *you* come to *me*?' he asked. 'I am the one who needs to be made clean, not you.'

But Jesus wanted John to baptize him, all the same. And as he came out of the water, he heard a voice, saying:

'You are my own dear Son. I am pleased with you.'

Put to the test

After this, Jesus spent forty days alone in the desert. When he was weak with hunger, Satan—God's enemy —began to test him. He was trying to make Jesus disobey God, to spoil his work.

'You are hungry. Turn these stones into loaves of bread.'

But Jesus refused. God had given him special powers. But he was not to use them selfishly.

'Kneel down. Worship me—and I will give you the wealth of the world.'

Again Jesus refused.

'God says we must worship him—and no one else,' he answered.

Satan tried all his tricks. But he could not make Jesus disobey God. At the end of the forty days Jesus set out for home. He was ready, now, for the work that lay ahead.

Jesus' work begins

When Jesus went back to Galilee, he did not go alone. He had already won his first followers.

Andrew had been with John the Baptist. He brought his brother, Peter, to meet Jesus. Andrew and Peter were fishermen from Lake Galilee. Philip came from the same home town. And he, in turn, brought Nathanael to Jesus.

Back in Galilee, Jesus left the carpenter's shop where he had worked. His real life's work was about to begin. Jesus had a message from God to share with the people.

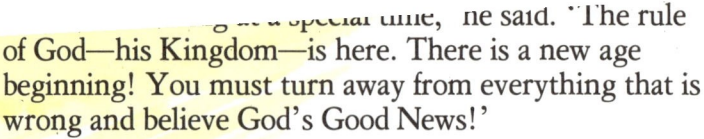

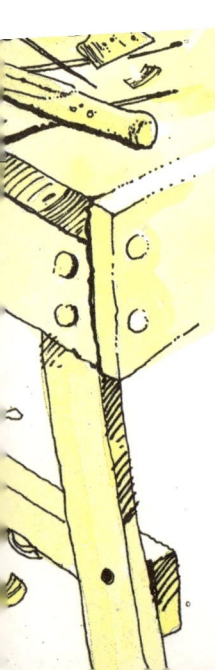

... a special time,' he said. 'The rule of God—his Kingdom—is here. There is a new age beginning! You must turn away from everything that is wrong and believe God's Good News!'

But people would not listen to him at home in Nazareth.

'Who does that carpenter think he is?' they muttered. 'You can't be a teacher unless you're trained!'

When he spoke in the synagogue—where the boys were taught their lessons during the week, and services were held on Saturdays, the Sabbath—they threw him out.

So Jesus went to the villages and towns nearby, where people were eager to listen.

Jesus goes to a wedding

There was a wedding at Cana in Galilee. Jesus' mother was there, helping. And Jesus and his friends were invited as guests. But the wine ran out before the wedding feast was over. Mary went and told Jesus.

'Do whatever he tells you,' she said to the servants.

There were six enormous water-jars standing near, so that people could wash before the meal, as the Jewish law said. But now they were empty.

'Fill them up,' Jesus said. And the servants filled them to the brim.

'Now pour some water out and take it to the man in charge of the feast.'

The servants looked at one another in dismay. But they did as Jesus said. When the man in charge tasted it, he said to the bridegroom:

'Everyone else serves the best wine first and keeps the ordinary wine for later. But you have kept the best until now.'

The water had changed into wine! This was the first of many wonderful things that Jesus did. And when his friends saw it, they began to believe the things he said.

The twelve friends

Everyone who heard Jesus was amazed at his teaching. It was all so new. And he spoke with such authority. When he began to heal those who were ill, the news spread like wildfire.

People came from far and near, and Jesus was busy from morning till night. He never had a moment to himself. Wherever he went, crowds gathered. He was often tired. But he never turned people away.

One day there was such a crowd on the lake-shore that Jesus stepped into Peter's boat.

'Row me a little way out,' he said. And he taught the people from there.

Afterwards Jesus told Peter to go out further, and let down the nets for a catch.

'We worked hard all night,' Peter said, 'and we didn't catch a thing. But if you say so . . .'

Peter and Andrew let down the nets—and caught so many fish that the nets were breaking!

'Come and help us,' they shouted to their partners, James and John, in the second boat. And they filled both boats with the catch.

'Now,' Jesus said, as they rowed for the shore, 'I want you to leave your fishing and come with me. From now on you'll be catching people!'

Not all of Jesus friends were fishermen. One day Jesus went out and saw a tax collector called Matthew, sitting in his office.

'Follow me!' Jesus said. And Matthew did!

Men like Matthew collected tax from the Jews to pay the Romans. They often grew rich by charging far more than they should have done. So it wasn't surprising they were hated and despised.

Matthew gave a feast for Jesus at his house. The religious people were shocked that Jesus went.

'Fancy mixing with people like that,' they said.

'I'm like a doctor,' Jesus answered. 'I treat people who are ill, not those who are well. I have come to bring these men and women back to God.'

At night, when the crowds went home, Jesus often went up into the hills to a lonely place where he could be quiet and pray. Sometimes he prayed all night. After a long night of prayer, Jesus chose twelve of his loyal followers to be his special friends:

Peter and Andrew; James and John; Philip and Bartholomew (Nathanael); Matthew; Thomas; James (son of Alphaeus); Simon; Judas, and Judas Iscariot (who later betrayed him).

These twelve men went everywhere with Jesus. They were his closest friends and he was their teacher. They saw the wonderful things he did. And he explained to them what God had sent him to do.

Lessons out of doors

On the Sabbath Jesus taught in the synagogues. But most of the time he taught out of doors. (Summers are long and hot and dry in Israel.) Out on the hills around Lake Galilee there was plenty of room for the crowds who came to hear him. He sat on the grass, with his followers all around him, listening.

He talked about happiness.

'You think rich people are the happy ones,' he said, 'because they have everything they want. But you are wrong.'

He looked at his followers. They were poor. Some
of them were hungry. But as citizens of God's
Kingdom they would have everything.

'Happy are you, poor,' Jesus said,
'the Kingdom of God is yours!
'Happy are you who are hungry now:
  you are going to be full!
'Happy are you who cry now:
  you are going to laugh!
'Happy are you when men hate and reject you
  for being my friends. A great reward is waiting
  for you in heaven.'

Jesus could see that the people were puzzled. So he
went on:

'Don't try to hoard money, or buy lots of things.
Someone will only steal them. Store up your treasure
with God, where no one can rob you. You have to
choose. Will you spend your life getting rich? Or will
you do what God wants? You can't do both.

'You are all such worriers. You worry about what
you are going to eat and what you are going to wear.
But there's more to life than food and clothes. Look at
the birds flying overhead. God takes care of them—and
he cares much more about you!

'Look around you. See how God dresses the wild
flowers! Not even the famous King Solomon had
clothes as beautiful as theirs. So don't spend your life
worrying. Do what God wants and he will give you all
you need. You can trust him!'

High standards

Jesus used picture-words to help them understand his teaching.

'You are like salt,' he said. 'Salt adds flavour and stops food going bad. You are to stop the rot in God's world, and make it taste good!

'You are like lamps. You must let your lives shine out in the darkness. Then, when people see the kind things you do, they will thank God.'

He talked about the kind of life God expects his people to live.

'You have God's laws in the Old Testament,' he said. 'But you are always trying to make them easier. God sets high standards. He tells you not to murder—and you obey him. But being angry—so angry you could kill someone—is wrong, too.

'You think it's fair to pay people back when they hurt you: an eye for an eye, or a tooth for a tooth. But God wants his people to *love* their enemies—to repay wrongs with kindness.

'It isn't easy to travel God's road. It's a hard path, and the gate at the entrance is narrow. But you must go through it and start on the journey.'

The prayer of Jesus

Then Jesus talked about giving to those in need.

'When you help people, keep quiet about it,' he said. 'Don't boast.'

'And don't show off or try to impress when you pray,' Jesus said. 'Find somewhere quiet. Talk to God as a father. And don't ask him for the same thing over and over again. He knows all your needs.

'This is how you should pray:

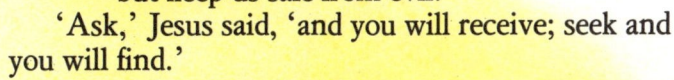

"Our Father in heaven:
may your name be honoured;
May your Kingdom come;
may your will be done on earth as it
is in heaven.
Give us today the food we need.
Forgive us the wrongs we have done,
as we forgive others the wrongs they
have done to us.
Do not bring us to the test,
but keep us safe from evil."

'Ask,' Jesus said, 'and you will receive; seek and you will find.'

The two house builders

Jesus had been talking for a long time. He finished with a story.

'Once upon a time two men decided to build themselves houses.

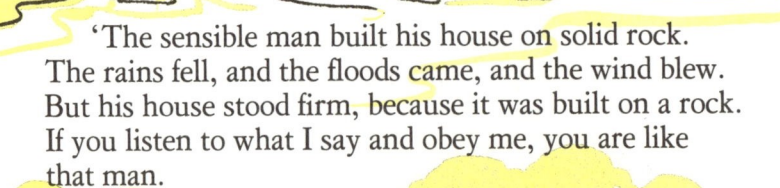

'The sensible man built his house on solid rock. The rains fell, and the floods came, and the wind blew. But his house stood firm, because it was built on a rock. If you listen to what I say and obey me, you are like that man.

'The silly man built his house on sand. It was easy to dig! But the rain fell and the floods came and the wind blew—and his house fell down with a great crash! If you listen to what I say but take no notice, you are just as silly as he was.'

The paralysed man

'Have you heard about the Teacher from Nazareth?
They say he can cure all kinds of illness.'

In those days, when only the rich could afford a
doctor, the news spread fast. Wherever Jesus went, sick
people came to him—and he made them well.

He cured the blind.

He cured the deaf.

He cured the dumb.

There was no illness of mind or body that Jesus
could not cure. God gave him special power to heal.
And when they saw what he could do, people began to
believe what Jesus said.

There was one man who was paralysed. His friends were sure Jesus could cure him. But he couldn't move. So four of his friends picked him up and carried him to Jesus on his bed-mat.

There was a crush outside the house where Jesus was teaching. No one could get in. So the four friends carried the man up the outside stairs to the flat roof. Then they broke through the layer of matting and plaster over the wooden beams, and lowered their friend down. Jesus looked up at the four men. How loving they were, and what faith they had!

'Your sins are forgiven,' he said to the man.

'Only God can forgive sins. How dare he!' muttered the teachers of the law.

'Which is easiest,' Jesus asked, 'to cure paralysis, or to forgive sins? I said it so that you would know I have God's power to do both.' Then he said to the man:

'Get up, pick up your mat, and go home.'

And to the delight of his friends, he did!

The storm

It was a calm evening. The lake was peaceful and sti.
Jesus and his followers got into the boat to cross to th.
other side. Jesus had not had a moment to himself all
day. He was very tired, and soon fell asleep.

Then, with no warning, a strong wind began to
blow. In no time the water was whipped into angry
waves. The little boat tossed. The men struggled with
the oars. But Jesus slept on.

The storm grew worse. The waves broke over the
sides of the boat, and it began to fill with water. The
men weren't easily frightened. They were fishermen.
They'd seen plenty of storms in their time. But now it
seemed as if nothing could save them. How could Jesus
sleep through it all?

They shook him awake.

'Wake up! Wake up!' they shouted. 'We're going
to drown!'

Jesus stood up. He spoke to the howling wind and
the steep-pitched waves!

'Be still!' he commanded.

And there was calm.

Then he said to his followers: 'Where is your
faith?'

No one said a word. They had been afraid of the
storm. Now they felt a little afraid of Jesus. He looked
like any normal man. And yet the wind and waves
obeyed his orders.

'Who can he really be?' they whispered to one
another.

Visit to Jerusalem

Each Spring, Jesus went to Jerusalem for the Passover Festival. The people there crowded to hear him teach.

The secret visitor
Nicodemus was a teacher, too. He had heard a lot about Jesus, and wanted to talk to him. But he didn't want people to see him—so he came after dark.

'We know you've been sent by God,' Nicodemus began. 'No one could do the wonderful things you do without God's help.'

Jesus knew the questions in Nicodemus's mind.

'You are a great teacher,' Jesus said. 'But you still have lessons to learn. You want to please God. But being good isn't enough. You must be born all over again to enjoy God's Kingdom.'

'What do you mean?' Nicodemus asked.

'You need a fresh start, a whole new life,' Jesus answered '—the life I have come to bring. You see, God loves the world so much that he has sent his Son. Everyone who puts his trust in me can have this new kind of life.'

Outside it was dark. Inside the house, the lamp shone.

'God's light is shining in the world,' Jesus said. 'But people would rather live in the dark—because the light shows up the wrong they do.'

The woman at the well

A few days later, the sun blazed down on Jesus and his friends as they began the long walk home to Galilee. When they reached the little town of Sychar, in Samaria, Jesus' friends went to buy food. It was midday. Jesus sat by the well, resting. It was very deep. He longed for a cup of cold water.

Soon a Samaritan woman came to the well. In those days the Jews weren't on speaking terms with the Samaritans. They certainly never used the same cups. So the woman was surprised when Jesus asked her to give him a drink.

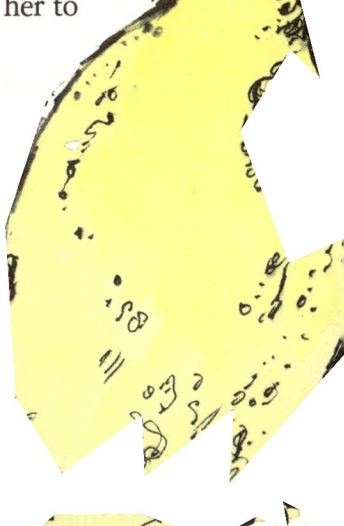

'If you knew what God can give, and who I am,' Jesus said, 'you would ask him for life-giving water, and never be thirsty again.'

'I would like that,' the woman answered. 'Then I need not come to the well. But where is the water? You have no bucket.'

'You don't understand,' Jesus said. 'I don't mean ordinary water to drink. I am talking about a new kind of life—the life I have come to bring.'

They had never met before. But the woman discovered that Jesus knew everything about her. She was so excited by what he said that she left her water-jar by the well! She hurried into the town to spread the good news.

'Come and meet this man,' she said. 'Do you think he could be God's promised King?'

Jesus' friends returned with the food. Soon they could see people hurrying towards them.

'The crops are ripe and ready for harvest,' Jesus said, as he watched them come.

He stayed in the town for two days. And when they heard his message, many of the Samaritans believed that he really was God's King—sent to save the world.

Trouble about the Sabbath

The ordinary people loved Jesus—and he loved them. Some left work and home and family to follow him.

Jesus had many friends, but he soon had enemies too. Some of the religious leaders and teachers were jealous because he was so popular.

One Sabbath day, at harvest time, Jesus and his friends were walking through the fields. They were hungry, so they picked some ears of wheat and ate them. The Pharisees—a strict religious sect, who took great pride in keeping every detail of the Jewish law—were shocked.

'You are breaking the law,' they said. 'That's work—and no one must work on the Sabbath.'

'God says, "It is kindness that I want," ' Jesus answered. 'You are wrong to condemn people when they're not guilty.'

Jesus went on to the local synagogue. There was a man there with a paralysed hand. People were watching to see if Jesus would heal him. That, too, would count as 'work'.

'What does our law allow us to do on the Sabbath?' Jesus asked. 'To help, or to harm? To save a man's life or to destroy it? You would rescue a sheep from a pit on the Sabbath day. Aren't people more important?'

'Stretch out your hand,' he said to the man. And the man's hand became strong and well again.

Another time, in Jerusalem, Jesus saw a man lying on his mat at the edge of a pool called Bethesda. He had been ill for thirty-eight years.

'Do you want to get well?' Jesus asked him. 'Then get up. Pick up your mat, and walk!'

Because it was the Sabbath, the man got into trouble with the Jewish authorities for carrying his mat! They came to see Jesus.

'God is always at work,' Jesus said to them. 'And I must work too.'

This made them even angrier. Jesus was breaking the law. Worse still, he was making himself out to be God's equal.

King Herod's birthday

John the Baptist was in trouble. King Herod Antipas*
had divorced his own wife to marry Herodias, the wife
of his half-brother, Philip. And John had told him
plainly it was wrong. So Herod had John arrested and
flung into prison. Herodias wanted to kill John, but
Herod was afraid. He knew that John was a good man.

Then King Herod had a birthday—and Herodias
got her chance. Her daughter danced to entertain the
guests at Herod's party. The king was so delighted he
promised her anything she cared to ask for—even half
his kingdom!

'Ask him for the head of John, on a dish,' Herodias
told her. And the girl obeyed.

Herod was very sad. He had made a silly promise.
And now he wouldn't break it. Not in front of all his
guests. So a guard was sent to the prison, and he cut off
John's head.

When John's friends heard, they came for the body
and buried it.

Then they went to tell Jesus.

*Son of Herod the Great, who was king when Jesus was born.

Believing—and forgiving

The Jews hated the Roman soldiers. But not all of them were bad. The Roman officer at Capernaum was good to the local people. He even had a synagogue built at his own expense.

Now his servant was dying. The soldier sent his Jewish friends to ask if Jesus would heal him.

'This Roman is a good man,' they told Jesus. 'He loves our people. Please help him.' So Jesus went with them.

When they were nearly at the house, the officer sent a message.

'I don't expect you to come in,' he said. 'Just give the order and my servant will get well. I am a soldier. I'm used to giving orders—and obeying them.'

Jesus was amazed when he heard this.

'I have not found faith like this before—even among the Jews,' he said.

The messengers returned—and found the officer's servant well again. Jesus had done what the Roman soldier asked.

Some time later, Jesus was invited to dinner by Simon the Pharisee.

As they reclined at the table, Roman style, a woman came in uninvited from the street. She carried a jar of scented oil, and she was crying.

She stood close to Jesus and her tears washed his dusty feet. She dried them with her long hair—and bathed them with the scented oil.

Simon was ashamed and embarrassed. The woman had a bad name. How could Jesus let her touch him?

Jesus knew what he was thinking.

'Simon,' he said, 'who is most grateful to be let off a debt, the man who owes a lot, or the man who owes only a little?'

The answer was obvious.

'You all need God to forgive you for something. But it's the ones who are forgiven most (like this woman) who love him most.'

Jesus said to the woman:

'Your sins are forgiven. Your faith has saved you. Go in peace.'

The good shepherd

When Jesus spoke, everyone listened. Even the children were quiet, hoping for a story. Jesus often used stories (parables) when he spoke about things that were hard to understand. He wanted people to think about them. If they really wanted to follow him, they would work out what the stories meant.

'If you have ears,' he often said, 'then listen.' He meant, 'Think hard, and try to understand.'

Jesus told his stories about familiar everyday things. On the brown hills of Israel were little flocks of sheep in the care of their shepherds.

'If one of you has a hundred sheep,' Jesus said, 'and one of them wanders away and gets lost, what does the shepherd do? He leaves the ninety-nine sheep who are safe, and sets out to find the one that is lost.

'He listens for its cry.

'He searches all the places where a sheep might stray, or get stuck, or hurt itself. It doesn't matter how tired he is, or how long it takes. He doesn't give up till he finds his lost sheep.

'And when he does, he's very happy. He picks the sheep up and carries it home. Then he calls his friends together.

' "Come and join the celebration," he says. "For I have found my lost sheep."

'There is joy like that in heaven,' Jesus said, '—over people. I have come to look for those who have wandered away from God, and bring them back home.'

'I am the good shepherd,' Jesus said. 'He never leaves his flock. He finds them fresh grass and leads them to water. He knows every one of his sheep. And he doesn't run off when a wolf attacks. The sheep follow their shepherd because they know his voice.

'I am the good shepherd. Those who follow me are my flock. They know me and they trust me. I lead and protect them. And I am ready to die for them.'

Alive and well!

Jesus was always kind to those in trouble. One day Jairus, one of the leaders in the local synagogue, came to ask for help.

'My little girl is very ill,' he said. 'I think she's dying. Please come.'

So Jesus set out for Jairus's house, and a crowd of people went with them.

There was a woman in the crowd who had been to one doctor after another for twelve years. But none of them had been able to stop the bleeding which was making her so ill. Jesus was her only hope.

'If I can just touch his clothes,' she said, 'I know I shall get well.'

As soon as she was close enough, she touched his coat. And the bleeding stopped.

'Who touched my coat?' Jesus asked. It seemed an odd question, with people crowding in all round. But Jesus knew that someone had been healed.

The woman came forward, nervously, and told him what she had done.

'Your faith has made you well,' Jesus said. 'Go in peace.'

That minute, messengers came from Jairus's house.

'Don't bother the teacher any longer, your daughter has died,' they told him.

'Don't be afraid,' Jesus said to Jairus, 'only believe, and she will get well.'

When they came to the house, everyone was weeping and wailing and making a great noise because the little girl was dead.

'Don't cry,' Jesus said. 'She's not dead—only asleep.' Then he went to the child's room, with Peter and James and John, and the little girl's parents.

Jesus took her by the hand, and said, 'Get up!' She got up at once.

'Give her something to eat,' Jesus said.

Her mother and father could hardly believe what had happened. But they were very glad indeed to have their little girl alive and well again.

God's Kingdom

Jesus came to offer everyone a new life in God's Kingdom. God himself is like a good king. His people will be happy. In his Kingdom there will be no sin and no death. One day it will all be perfect. And it is beginning now! Jesus told a great many stories to show what God's Kingdom is like.

The sower

'There was a farmer who went out to sow his corn,' Jesus began. 'As he sowed the seed, some fell on the path. But the birds soon pecked it up. Some fell on shallow stony soil. And the hot sun shrivelled the growing plants, because their roots weren't deep. Some fell among thistles and weeds and they smothered it. But some fell on good soil and produced corn.'

Then Jesus explained the story.

'It is like that with God's message and those who hear it,' he said. 'The Evil One may come and snatch it away. Or people may listen gladly, but give up when trouble comes. Others let their worries or their love of money smother the message. But there are those, like the seeds sown in good soil, who hear and understand. Their lives show how they've taken God's message to heart.'

The weeds

Jesus told another story.

'A farmer ploughed his land and sowed wheat. The seed was good. But the farmer had an enemy. When everyone was asleep, his enemy came and sowed weeds among the wheat. No one knew, until the seeds came up and began to grow.

' "Shall we pull up the weeds?" his servants asked.

' "No," said the farmer, "you might uproot some of the wheat. Let both grow till harvest. Then we'll pull up the weeds and burn them, and store the wheat in my barn." '

When the crowds had gone home, Jesus' friends asked him to tell them what the story meant.

'I am the sower,' Jesus said. 'The field is the world. The good seeds are the people who belong to God; the weeds are those who belong to God's enemy, the Evil One. The harvest will come at the end of time.'

The mustard seed

'There was a man who took a tiny mustard seed,' Jesus said, 'and planted it in his field. It was so small it was like a speck of dust. But the little seed grew. Soon it was a strong plant. It grew and grew till it was like a great tree. The birds built their nests in its branches.

'God's Kingdom is like that—growing and growing.'

Buried treasure

'A man digging in a field found buried treasure. He was very excited. But he did not own the land, so he covered the treasure with soil. He went away and sold everything he had. Then he bought the land, and the treasure was his.

'Make sure that God's Kingdom is yours!'

The pearl

'There was a merchant who bought and sold pearls. A man came to him one day with the finest pearl the merchant had ever seen—it was so big, and so beautiful. The merchant knew he would never be happy until the pearl was his. So he sold everything he had, and bought it.

'God's Kingdom is like that: worth more than anything else.'

The hungry crow

It was another busy day, with no time even to eat. A crowd of people had been listening to Jesus. Now the sun was going down, and everyone was hungry.

'Send the people away to buy food,' Jesus' friends said.

'No,' Jesus answered. 'We must give them something to eat. How much bread have you got?'

Andrew, Peter's brother, said:

'There's a boy here with five barley loaves and two small fish. But that won't go far.'

'Tell everyone to sit down on the grass,' Jesus said. (There was a crowd of about 5,000.)

Then Jesus took the boy's bread and fish and thanked God for them. His friends took the food round—and to their great surprise everyone had enough to eat. The left-overs filled twelve baskets.

Next day, Jesus spoke of another kind of bread.

'I am the bread of life,' he said. 'Come to me and I will give you all that you need for the new life I have come to bring.'

On the mountain

The crowds had heard Jesus teach. They had seen the wonderful things he did.

'Who do they say I am?' Jesus asked his twelve friends one day.

'Some say you're John the Baptist come back to life— or one of the prophets,' they answered.

'And what about you? Who do *you* think I am?'

Peter answered for them all. He was quite sure.

'You are the promised King, the Son of the living God.'

Jesus was pleased with Peter's answer. Now he could tell his friends about some of the things that lay ahead. He must prepare them.

'Soon,' he said, 'I must go to Jerusalem. But they won't accept me as God's King. They will put me to death. But after three days I shall live again.'

Jesus told his friends that they must expect to suffer, too.

'If anyone wants to come with me,' he said, 'he must take up his cross and follow me.'

About a week later, Jesus took Peter and James and John with him up a high mountain, to pray. While they were there, a change came over him: his face and clothes became dazzling bright. Two other shining figures came and talked to him. They were Moses, and the prophet Elijah. They talked to Jesus about his death.

The three friends had fallen asleep. When they woke up and saw all this, they were frightened.

Then a cloud came over, and a voice from the cloud:

'This is my Son—listen to him!'

And they were alone again on the mountain with Jesus.

The two sons

It wasn't just good people who came to hear Jesus. He mixed with the kind of people no one else would speak to. The Pharisees grumbled about the company he kept.
  So one day he told them this story.

There was once a man who had two sons. The younger one asked to have his share of the property. When he got it, he left home. He went on a spending spree abroad. When he had no money left, there was a terrible shortage of food. People were starving. He got a job on a pig farm. He was so hungry he could have eaten the bean pods he fed to the pigs!

He was homesick, too.
  'This is very silly,' he thought. 'My father's workmen have more than enough to eat. And here am I, starving! I'll go home. I'll tell my father how sorry I am for all I've done. I'm not fit to be his son. But perhaps he'll take me on as one of his men.'

So he started back. His father saw him coming and ran out to meet him. He threw his arms around his son and hugged him!

'Bring him some new clothes,' he called to his servants. 'And kill the prize calf. We must hold a great feast to celebrate. I thought my son was dead, but he's alive after all.'

When the elder son came home, he was furious!

'I've worked for you all these years, and you've never given *me* a feast,' he said to his father. 'Yet you kill the prize calf for my no-good brother.'

'You know that everything I have is yours,' his father said. 'We had to celebrate and be happy. Your brother was lost, but now he's been found.'

The Pharisees and their questions

The Pharisees and religious leaders were jealous and afraid of Jesus. They hated him and wanted him out of the way. So they set traps for him by asking catch questions. But Jesus always had an answer.

The good Samaritan

'Teacher,' one of them asked, 'what must I do to receive the new life?'

'What does God's law tell you?' Jesus answered.

'To love God with all my heart and mind and strength,' the man replied. 'And to love my neighbour as much as myself.'

'That's right,' said Jesus.

'But what does it mean?' the man asked. 'Who is my neighbour?'

So Jesus told him this story.

'A man was travelling down the road from Jerusalem to Jericho. In a lonely place, bandits attacked him. They robbed him of his money and beat him up.

'After a little while a priest came by. He saw the man lying there, but did nothing to help. He just walked past, on the other side of the road.

'Then a teacher of God's law came along. He went and looked at the man. But he didn't help him, either.

'But a Samaritan, travelling down the road, stopped when he saw the injured man. He gently washed and bandaged his cuts, put the man on his own donkey and took him to the nearest inn. Next day, when he had to leave, he gave the inn-keeper some money.

' "Take good care of him" he said. "And if it costs you more than this, I'll pay you when I come back." He did all this for a stranger and a foreigner—a Jew who despises Samaritans.'

Jesus turned to the man who had asked the question.

'Now which of these people was a good neighbour to the man who was hurt?'

'The one who was kind to him.'

'Go, then,' Jesus said, 'and be like him.'

The Pharisee and the tax collector

Jesus told this story to the goody-goody people who looked down their noses at others.

'Two men went to God's Temple to pray. One was a Pharisee, the other a tax collector.

'This is how the Pharisee prayed:

' "I thank you, God, that I'm not greedy, like other people. And I'm not a cheat—like that tax collector over there. I do all that your law commands. I even give you a tenth of all I earn."

'The tax collector hung his head, he was so ashamed of himself.

' "O God, take pity on a sinner," he said.

'I tell you,' Jesus said, 'it was the tax collector, not the Pharisee, who was right with God when he went home. For everyone who makes himself out to be great will be made small. And everyone who thinks little of himself will be made great.

Jesus and the children

People brought their babies to Jesus, asking him to pray
for them. Jesus' friends tried to stop them. But he said:
'Let the children come to me. Don't stop them. God's
Kingdom belongs to people who are like these children.
Anyone who wants to enter God's Kingdom must
come to·him like a little child.'

Martha, Mary and Lazarus

When Jesus went to Jerusalem, he often stayed with his friends—Martha and Mary and their brother Lazarus. They lived at Bethany, about two miles from the city.

Martha was always busy with the cooking and housework. She was good at it. Mary was the quiet one. When Jesus came to stay, she somehow forgot about the work as she listened to him. This made Martha cross.

'Tell Mary to come and help me!' she said to Jesus.

'Martha,' he said, 'don't fuss. You are worrying about too many things. A simple meal will do. Mary is right to listen to me while she can.'

One day the sisters sent Jesus a message:
'Lazarus is very ill.'

They knew how Jesus loved them all. And they expected him to come straight away. But instead he stayed where he was for two days. He knew by then that Lazarus was dead—but God had a special purpose in all this.

'Let's go now,' Jesus said to the twelve.

'It's dangerous,' they said. 'You have too many enemies in Jerusalem.'

But Jesus clearly meant to go, so Thomas said: 'Let's all go with him—then we can die together!'

When Jesus arrived, Lazarus had been in the grave for four days. Martha came out to meet him.

'If only you'd been here,' Martha said, 'my brother would not have died.'

'He will live again,' Jesus said.

'I know he will, when God brings all the dead back to life at the resurrection,' Martha answered.

'I am the resurrection and the life,' Jesus said to her. 'Whoever believes in me will live, even though he dies.'

Martha told Mary that Jesus was asking for her—and she hurried out, crying.

'If only you'd been here, my brother wouldn't have died,' she said to Jesus, just as Martha had done.

When Jesus saw her tears, and saw all their friends and neighbours crying too, he wept.

Everyone could see how much he had loved Lazarus. They wondered more than ever why he had not come sooner.

Jesus led them to the grave.

'Take the entrance stone away,' he ordered.

Martha protested: 'He's been in there four days. The body will smell!'

'Didn't I tell you that, if you believed, you would see God's glory?' Jesus said.

He prayed. And then he called in a loud voice:

'Lazarus, come out!'

Lazarus came, still wrapped from head to foot in the grave clothes they wound round dead bodies in those days.

'Unwrap him and set him free,' Jesus said.

The people who saw it believed that Jesus had been sent to them by God. But when the Pharisees and the chief priests in Jerusalem heard what had happened, they held a meeting.

'If we don't put a stop to this,' they said, 'everyone will believe in Jesus. The Romans will suspect a rebellion—and they will destroy us all.'

From that day on, they made plans to kill Jesus.

On the way to Jerusalem

Jesus was on his way to Jerusalem for the last time. As he and his friends went into a village, they met ten men.

They were suffering from a terrible skin disease. It disfigured their hands and faces. Because of it, the men had had to leave their families and live on their own outside the village.

Now they stood a little way off and called out to Jesus: 'Take pity on us!'

When he saw them, Jesus said:

'Go to the priest and let him examine you.' (They could not go home unless the priest said they were cured.)

On the way, their skin healed and they were completely well again.

One man, a Samaritan, came straight back to thank Jesus. The rest were in too much of a hurry to get home.

'Ten men were healed. Where are the other nine?' Jesus asked. 'Why is this foreigner the only one who came back to say thank you to God?'

Blind Bartimaeus

Bartimaeus lived in Jericho. He was blind, so he could not work for his living. Instead he sat at the dusty roadside, day after day, begging for food and money from passers-by.

He longed to be able to see, and go to work, and enjoy life like other people. He had heard stories of how Jesus could cure all kinds of illness. And he made up his mind that if ever Jesus came to Jericho he would ask his help.

Then, one day, Jesus came.

Bartimaeus could hear the noise of a great crowd of people coming along the road.

'What is it? What is it?' he asked. 'Tell me what you can see!'

'It's Jesus,' they told him. 'He's coming this way.'

Bartimaeus could not see. But there was nothing wrong with his voice! He began to shout:

'Jesus of Nazareth! Take pity on me!'

He made so much noise that people got cross with him. But he kept on shouting.

Jesus called Bartimaeus to him. The blind beggar jumped up, threw off his coat and came.

'What do you want me to do for you?' Jesus asked him.

'I want to see again,' Bartimaeus answered.

'So you shall,' Jesus said. 'Your faith has made you well.'

At once Bartimaeus was able to see. He could see Jesus! Joyfully he joined the crowd that followed him.

Zacchaeus

The chief tax collector in Jericho was a man called Zacchaeus. He was very rich. But he wasn't much to look at. He was a small man.

He wanted to see Jesus, but there were too many people in front of him. He was almost in despair, when he had an idea. He ran ahead of the crowd and climbed a tree! It wasn't very dignified—but he had a fine view.

Jesus walked right under his tree. He looked up and said to Zacchaeus:

'Come down, Zacchaeus. I'm going to stay at your house today.'

Zacchaeus nearly fell off his branch in surprise. He could hardly believe his ears.

He was overjoyed to welcome Jesus to his home.

From that day on, Zacchaeus was a changed man.

'I will give half my money to the poor,' he said. 'And if I've cheated anyone, I'll pay him back four times as much.'

The King rides in

Jesus was close to Jerusalem now. He wanted to be there for the Passover Festival. Jesus spoke to two of his friends.

'Go ahead to the next village,' he said. 'You'll find a donkey tied up there. It has never been ridden. Untie it and bring it to me. If anyone asks what you're doing, tell them I sent you.'

The two men brought the donkey to Jesus. Then they threw their coats across the donkey's back and helped Jesus to mount.

People were crowding into Jerusalem. As soon as they heard Jesus was coming, they came out to meet him. Some of them spread their coats on the road in front of him. Others cut branches of palm.

'Here comes God's King,' they shouted. 'Praise God!'

So Jesus rode into the city like a King—but one who comes in peace.

He went to the Temple, and when he saw the men selling pigeons for sacrifice, and money-changers giving out the special Temple coins, he was very angry. They were cheating people who had come to worship God.

'God's Temple is a place of prayer,' Jesus cried. 'But you have made it into a robber's den.' Then he overturned their tables and drove them out. The place was in an uproar.

The priests were angrier than ever. Jesus must be arrested—but how? They dared not risk a riot.

The last meal
—and betrayal!

Two days before the Passover, Judas Iscariot, one of the
twelve, went to see the chief priests. He was angry and
disappointed. He had expected Jesus to lead a revolt
against the Romans. Now Judas was ready to betray
him.

'I will lead you to him when there are no crowds
about,' he told the priests. And they paid him thirty
silver coins.

'Where shall we meet for the Passover meal?' asked
Jesus' friends, on the morning of the festival. It was
time to get things ready.

'Go into the city,' Jesus said. 'You'll see a man
carrying a jar of water. Follow him to his house. There
is an upstairs room where we can have our meal
together.'

That evening, before they sat down to eat, Jesus took a towel, poured some water into a basin, and began to wash their feet. This was a servant's job, and Peter was shocked.

Jesus explained. 'You must be willing to serve one another, just as I have served you,' he said.

Jesus knew he would not be with them much longer. He was going to die. The friends could see that something was wrong. Jesus looked so sad.

'One of you is going to betray me,' he said at last. They were stunned. No one said anything for a minute.

Then John, who was next to him, whispered to Jesus, 'Who is it?'

'The one to whom I give this piece of bread, dipped in the sauce,' Jesus answered.

He gave it to Judas.

'Go and do what you have to,' Jesus said to him. So Judas went out into the dark night.

Jesus talked a lot that evening, and his friends never

forgot his words. He told them how much he loved them—so much, he was going to die for them.

'I won't leave you on your own,' he said. 'God will send his Spirit to be with you and help you always. I am going back to God, to get a place ready for you. Then I will come and take you to be with me. Don't worry. And don't be afraid.'

Jesus took a loaf of bread, thanked God for the food, and shared it round.

'This is my body,' he said. 'I am going to be broken, like this bread—to die. And I will be dying for you.'

Then he took a cup of wine, gave God thanks, and they all shared it.

'This is my blood, poured out for many people. My death will seal the new peace between God and his people.'

When the meal was over, they left the house and walked to an orchard of olive-trees called Gethsemane.

Betrayed!

On the way there, Jesus tried to warn his friends what would happen.

'In just a few hours,' he said, 'you will all run away and leave me.'

'I never will!' said Peter.

But Jesus said: 'Before the cock crows at dawn, you will say three times that you do not know me.'

'I would die first!' Peter said. And they all agreed.

When they came to Gethsemane, Jesus took Peter, James and John in with him. The others sat down to wait.

'Come with me, and keep watch,' he said to the three. He was very upset. They moved in amongst the trees and Jesus knelt to pray.

'Father, if it's possible,' he said, 'save me from this death. But only if that's what *you* want.' Three times he prayed, and three times, when he went back to Peter, James and John, he found that they had fallen asleep.

The third time he woke them, they could hear voices. People were coming. Torches flared. The Temple guards, and the chief priests, led by Judas, had come to arrest Jesus.

'The one I kiss is the man you want,' Judas said to the soldiers. Then he went up to Jesus and kissed him. The soldiers closed in.

Jesus did not try to escape or to resist them.

But Peter drew his sword. He cut off the right ear of Malchus, the High Priest's servant.

'Put your sword away,' Jesus said to Peter. And he touched the man's ear and healed it.

Then he turned to the chief priests.

'Why have you come against me with swords and clubs, as if I were a criminal?' he asked.

There was no reply. The soldiers seized him roughly by the arms and marched him off.

Every one of his friends ran off and left him.

Sentenced to death

The soldiers took Jesus to the High Priest's house. Peter followed at a safe distance. There was a fire in the centre of the courtyard, and the guards stood round it. Peter joined them.

A servant girl walked past and saw him.

'You were with Jesus of Nazareth,' she said.

Peter denied it. He moved away. But she said to the others: 'This is one of Jesus' followers.'

'No. You are wrong. I'm not,' said Peter.

A little while later someone heard Peter's north-country voice.

'You come from Galilee,' he said. 'You must know Jesus.'

'I swear I've never met him,' Peter answered, sweating with fright.

Just then a cock crowed, and Peter remembered what Jesus had said. He broke down and cried.

Inside the house, Jesus was being tried by the Jewish Council. It was still dark when the High Priest's servants called them all together. They intended to put Jesus to death, but they wanted it to look like a fair trial. Witnesses were brought in—but none of their stories agreed.

At last the High Priest questioned the prisoner himself.

'Why don't you answer the charges?' he said.

But Jesus would not say a word.

Then the High Priest asked him, on oath, if he was the King, the Son of God.

'I am,' Jesus answered. 'You will all see me at God's side, coming with the clouds of heaven.'

'You have heard what the prisoner said. We need no more witnesses,' said the High Priest. 'He claims to be equal with God, and that is blasphemy. Do you find him guilty?'

'Yes, guilty,' they shouted. They sentenced him to death. But they needed the Roman governor's consent to carry out the execution. So, early in the morning, they took Jesus to Pontius Pilate.

When Judas heard that Jesus had been sentenced to death, he was bitterly sorry for what he had done. He went to the chief priests and threw the silver coins on the table. Then he went away and hanged himself.

Jesus stood before the Roman governor, Pontius Pilate. The Jewish priests accused him of treason, because they knew that Pilate would not sentence a man to death for blasphemy.

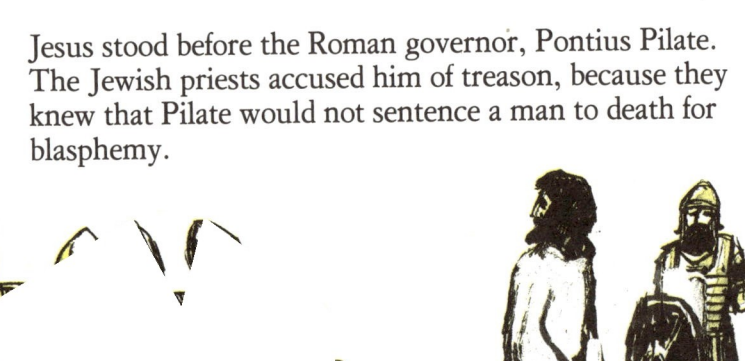

'He claimed to be a King,' they said.

So Pilate questioned Jesus. But he could find no reason to put him to death. Jesus had done no wrong. It was the custom at Passover to give one of the prisoners his freedom.

'I have not found this man guilty,' Pilate said. 'I shall set Jesus free.'

But the crowd, stirred up by the priests, would not let him.

'Kill Jesus!' they shouted. 'Crucify him! And free Barabbas.' (Barabbas was a murderer.)

They made such an uproar with their shouting that at last Pilate gave in. He knew it was wrong. But he was afraid the people would riot and get him into trouble with the Emperor.

'I am not responsible for the death of this man,' he said. 'It is your doing.'

Then he had Jesus flogged, and handed him over to his soldiers to be crucified. Crucifixion was the terrible slow death the Romans reserved for criminals.

The soldiers took Jesus away. They dressed him up as a king in a purple robe, with a cruel crown of thorn, and mocked him. They spat in his face. Then they took off the robe and led him through the city streets to Golgotha, the place of execution.

The cross

Jesus was weak from the flogging, but they made him carry the heavy wooden beam of the cross till he stumbled and fell. Then they ordered one of the crowd—a man called Simon, from Cyrene—to carry it for him.

At Golgotha, outside the city walls, they nailed Jesus' hands and feet to the cross.

There was a notice above Jesus' head:

'This is Jesus, the King of the Jews.'

The hot sun beat down and Jesus hung there, in great pain. Yet he did not hate his executioners.

'Forgive them, Father,' he prayed. 'They don't know what they are doing.'

'If you really are the Son of God,' jeered the people standing by, 'save yourself!'

Two thieves were crucified with Jesus, one on either side. The first thief sneered at him. But the second thief said: 'We deserve to die, but this man has done nothing wrong. Remember me, Jesus, when you come as King.'

Jesus answered, 'Today you will be with me in paradise—I promise.'

Jesus' mother and some of his friends stood near. Jesus spoke to John: 'Take my mother home,' he said, 'and look after her for me.'

At midday a shadow passed across the sun, and for three hours it was strangely dark.

'O God, why have you left me?' Jesus whispered.

Then he gave a great cry—'It is finished!'—and died.

At that moment the curtain in the Temple split from top to bottom. And the earth shook beneath the soldiers' feet. They had been tossing up for Jesus' clothes. Now they were terrified.

'This man really was the Son of God!' they said.

To make sure that Jesus was dead, one of the soldiers thrust his sword into Jesus' side. Then they took his body down from the cross.

A man called Joseph, from Arimathaea—a follower of Jesus—went to Pilate and asked if he could take Jesus' body away for burial. Pilate agreed. Joseph and Nicodemus (Jesus' secret visitor) wrapped the body in long strips of cloth, with myrrh and other spices.

Mary Magdalene and the other women who had followed Jesus from Galilee went with Joseph and saw him put the body in a new grave, a large cave dug out of rock. A heavy stone was rolled across the entrance. It was Friday, and the Sabbath began at sunset. So the women went away to prepare ointments and spices to put on the body when the Sabbath was over.

The Jewish authorities asked Pilate for a guard. They put a seal on the stone. And the guards settled down to keep watch.

Alive from the dead!

It was Sunday morning, just before dawn. Everything was still. Then, as the first light touched the sky, the ground trembled and shook. An angel came and rolled away the stone that sealed the tomb. The guards were so frightened, they ran off.

When the women came, bringing their spices, the grave was open and the body had gone. The angel spoke to them:

'Don't be afraid,' he said. 'I know you are looking for Jesus. But he's not here. He's alive from the dead! Look, this is where his body was. Hurry and tell his friends. You will see him again soon.'

Jesus' friends refused to believe the women's story. They thought they were imagining things! But Peter and John went to the grave, to see for themselves.

John ran faster than Peter, and got there first. He looked inside the grave, but didn't go in. Then Peter arrived and they both went in.

They saw the cloths which had bound the body, lying untouched, with the cloth that had wrapped Jesus' head just a neck-space away. John knew at once that no one could have stolen the body. What the women had said was true! Jesus *was* alive from the dead!

The two men went home. But Mary Magdalene, who had followed them, stayed. She stood there, crying. She could not understand what had happened. Then she caught sight of a man she thought was the gardener.

'If you have taken him away,' she said, 'please tell me where to find him.' She did not know she was talking to Jesus!

Then Jesus said, 'Mary!' She knew at once who it was. Joy flooded through her.

'Tell my friends you have seen me,' Jesus said.

Emmaus road

Later that day, a man called Cleopas and another of Jesus' followers were walking home to Emmaus, outside Jerusalem. As they were talking, a stranger caught up with them.

'Why are you so sad?' he asked.

'Are you the only person in Jerusalem who doesn't know what's been happening there these last few days?' Cleopas answered.

'Why, what's that?' he asked.

'About Jesus of Nazareth,' Cleopas replied. 'He was a great teacher. We all thought he was God's promised King. But they put him to death on Friday. Then this morning some women went to his grave. They said the body had gone, and that an angel had told them Jesus was alive!'

'Why are you so puzzled?' the stranger asked. 'Don't you know that the prophets said all this would happen?' And he began to explain.

When they got home, they asked him in.

'It's nearly dark. Come and have a meal with us.'

When the meal was ready, the visitor took the bread in his hands and thanked God for it. Then they knew that the stranger was Jesus—and no sooner did they recognize him, than he had gone.

In great excitement they hurried back to Jerusalem to tell their friends.

No ghost!

The eleven were all together, with other friends of Jesus. 'It *must* be true,' they said. 'Peter has seen him, too.'

The doors were locked. They were afraid. Suddenly, there was Jesus, standing in the room with them! They were terrified at first. They thought they were seeing a ghost! But Jesus calmed them down. He showed them the marks of the nails in his hands and feet. Then they knew it must be him.

'Touch me,' he said. 'Ghosts aren't made of flesh and bones.' Then they knew he was real.

Still they could hardly believe it was true. It was so good to see and talk to him again!

'Is there anything to eat?' Jesus asked.

They gave him some fish and watched him eat it. After that there were no more doubts. It *was* Jesus. He was real. He was alive!

Jesus explained how all that had happened was part of God's wonderful plan. He quoted from God's law, from the prophets and the psalms.

'God's King had to suffer and die,' he said, 'and live again. The penalty for sin has been paid. Death has been conquered. Now God offers a free pardon to everyone who believes and comes to him for new life. It's good news for people of every nation. And you will go and tell them.'

The doubter

Thomas was not with the others that evening. He refused to believe their story.

'Unless I see the nail-marks in his hands and touch the wound in his side,' Thomas said, 'I won't believe he's alive.'

A week later, they were together again. The doors were locked. Suddenly Jesus was there in the room.

'Look at the nail-marks in my hands,' he said to Thomas. 'Touch the sword-wound in my side. Stop doubting—and believe!'

But Thomas did not need to look or to touch. His doubts had gone.

'My Lord—and my God,' he said.

Breakfast by the lake

Over the next few weeks, many of Jesus' followers saw
him. His friends left Jerusalem and went back to
Galilee.

'I'm going fishing,' Peter said to the others, one
morning.

'We'll come too,' they said. So they went out in the
boat and fished all night. But they caught nothing.

At dawn, Jesus stood on the shore—but they did
not know it was him.

'Have you caught any fish?' he shouted.

'Nothing at all,' they said.

'Throw the net out now, and you'll make a catch.'

They threw out the net—and caught so many fish
they couldn't haul them in.

'It's Jesus,' John said to Peter.

Jesus had a fire lit already.

'Bring some of the fish you've just caught,' he said.
'And we'll have breakfast.'

After the meal, Jesus had a question for Peter.

'Do you love me?' he asked.

'Yes,' said Peter. 'You *know* I love you.'

Three times Jesus asked him the same question,
and three times Peter answered, 'You know I do.'

'Then take good care of my followers,' Jesus said.

Wind and fire!

Jesus and his friends were on the Mount of Olives, outside Jerusalem. The time had come for the final goodbye. It was nearly six weeks after Jesus' resurrection.

'Very soon,' Jesus said, 'God will send you his Spirit. He will help you to speak out bravely. You are to tell the people in Jerusalem, and Judea and Samaria—and the whole world—what I have done. Tell them the good news that everyone who trusts in me and is truly sorry for the wrong he's done will be forgiven. I will give him a new life!'

When he had said this, Jesus was taken up to heaven. As they watched, a cloud hid him. Suddenly, two men dressed in white were standing with them.

'Jesus has gone back to be with God,' they said. 'But one day he will return.'

On the Day of Pentecost (the Jewish festival at the beginning of harvest) Jesus' friends were together again, in a house in Jerusalem. Suddenly there was the sound of a strong wind blowing. Flames of fire touched each person.

God had sent his Spirit, as Jesus promised. They began to speak—not in their own language, but in languages they had never learnt!

Jerusalem was crowded with Jewish visitors for the Festival. They came from Egypt and north Africa, from Persia, Crete and Arabia. To their surprise, they heard these men telling them in their own languages about the wonderful things God had done.

Peter stood up to speak. 'Let me tell you about Jesus,' he said. He told them the wonderful things Jesus had said and done; how he had been put to death; how God had brought him to life again.

'You have done a terrible thing,' Peter said. 'You crucified God's promised King.'

'What can we do?' they asked.

'Ask God to forgive you. Begin a new life. Be baptized in the name of Jesus. And God will give you his Spirit. He will stay with you always, and help you.'

That day three thousand people became Christians.

The lame man —and a warning

Every day Jesus' friends and the new Christians met together in the Temple. Peter and the others were their teachers. They had meals together. And what money they had, they shared.

One day Peter and John went to the Temple to pray. At the gate they met a man who had been lame all his life. He was begging for money.

Peter spoke to him.

'I have no money to give you,' he said. 'But I can give you something better. In the name of Jesus, stand up, and walk!'

Peter put out a hand to help him up—and the man could feel his feet and ankles growing stronger! He could stand! He could walk! He could even jump!

'Thank you, oh, thank you God!' he said. All the people who saw him were amazed at what had happened.

The priests were angry with the friends of Jesus for telling everyone that Jesus was alive from the dead. Now they had made a lame man walk. The whole city was buzzing with the news. The priests sent guards to arrest Peter and John.

The two men stood before the Jewish Council.

'How were you able to heal the lame man?'

'Jesus made him well,' they replied.

'Never mention that name again!' the Council ordered them.

Peter and John knew that their lives were in danger. A few weeks before, they would have been scared. But God's own Spirit was with them now.

'Is it right to do what you tell us, or what God tells us?' they answered bravely. 'We can't stop talking about the things we have seen and heard.'

The Council made threats. Then they set Peter and John free. They went straight to their friends. And they began to pray. But they did not ask God to keep them safe. Instead, they asked him to help them speak out bravely. And God answered their prayer.

Stephen

People flocked to hear the friends of Jesus. They
brought those who were ill to be healed. Many of them
became Christians. They sold what they owned, and the
money was shared out. But it was difficult to be quite
fair, and there were quarrels.

So Jesus' friends chose seven men to sort things
out. One of them was Stephen, a man who really
trusted God.

But Stephen's enemies bribed men to bring a
charge against him.

'We heard him speaking against Moses and against
God,' they said.

Stephen was called before the Jewish Council. He
spoke to them about the history of Israel—about
Abraham and Jacob and Joseph. He came to the story
of Moses, and how the Israelites disobeyed God.

'Out there in the desert, and ever since,' he said,
'you have refused to hear God's message. Now you
have killed his Son.'

Stephen looked up—and his eyes widened:

'I can see Jesus now,' he said, 'standing beside
God!'

This was too much for the Council. They rushed at
Stephen and dragged him outside the city. Then they
hurled stones at him to kill him.

'Lord Jesus,' Stephen cried. 'Don't hold this crime
against them.' Then he died.

A young man called Paul was standing there watching. He threw no stones, but he approved of the killing. The Christians must be got rid of!

Paul was a Pharisee, proud of God's law. Although he was born in far-off Tarsus, he had studied in Jerusalem with the best teachers.

After Stephen's death, Paul led a house-to-house search for the Christians. Many were thrown into prison. Others escaped.

Philip went to Samaria and began to tell the people there about Jesus. One day God sent him to the Gaza road. A carriage was coming slowly towards him. In it sat a high official of the queen of Ethiopia. He was reading out loud from a book.

Philip knew those words!

'Do you understand what you are reading?' he asked.

'How can I, unless someone explains,' the man replied. And he invited Philip to join him. He was reading from the prophet Isaiah. The passage was one Jesus had often explained to his friends. It foretold his death. So Philip told the man the good news about Jesus. He wanted to become a Christian straight away! So Philip baptized him. And he went on his way, a happy man.

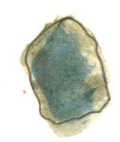

Paul joins the Christians

Paul left Jerusalem for Damascus in Syria. He had heard there was a group of Christians there. He was going to arrest them. But on the way, a strange thing happened. The sun blazed down. The light grew brighter and brighter—so bright that it was blinding! Paul stumbled and fell. He heard someone call his name.

'Paul! Paul! Why are you trying to kill me?'

'Who are you?' he asked.

'I am Jesus. Go into the city. When you are there, you will be told what to do.'

The men with Paul heard the voice. But they could not see anyone. Paul got up. He opened his eyes—but he couldn't see! He was blind. They took him by the hand, and led him into Damascus.

There was a Christian in Damascus called Ananias. God spoke to him in a vision.

'A man called Paul is staying at a house in Straight Street. I have told him you will place your hands on him and give him back his sight.'

'But this man has done terrible things to the Christians,' Ananias protested. 'And he's come here to arrest us.'

'I have chosen Paul to take my message to the nations of the world. I will show him all that he must suffer for my sake.'

So Ananias went to Paul.

'Jesus has sent me to you,' he said, 'so that you may see again, and receive God's Spirit.' And straight away, Paul could see—after three days in the dark!

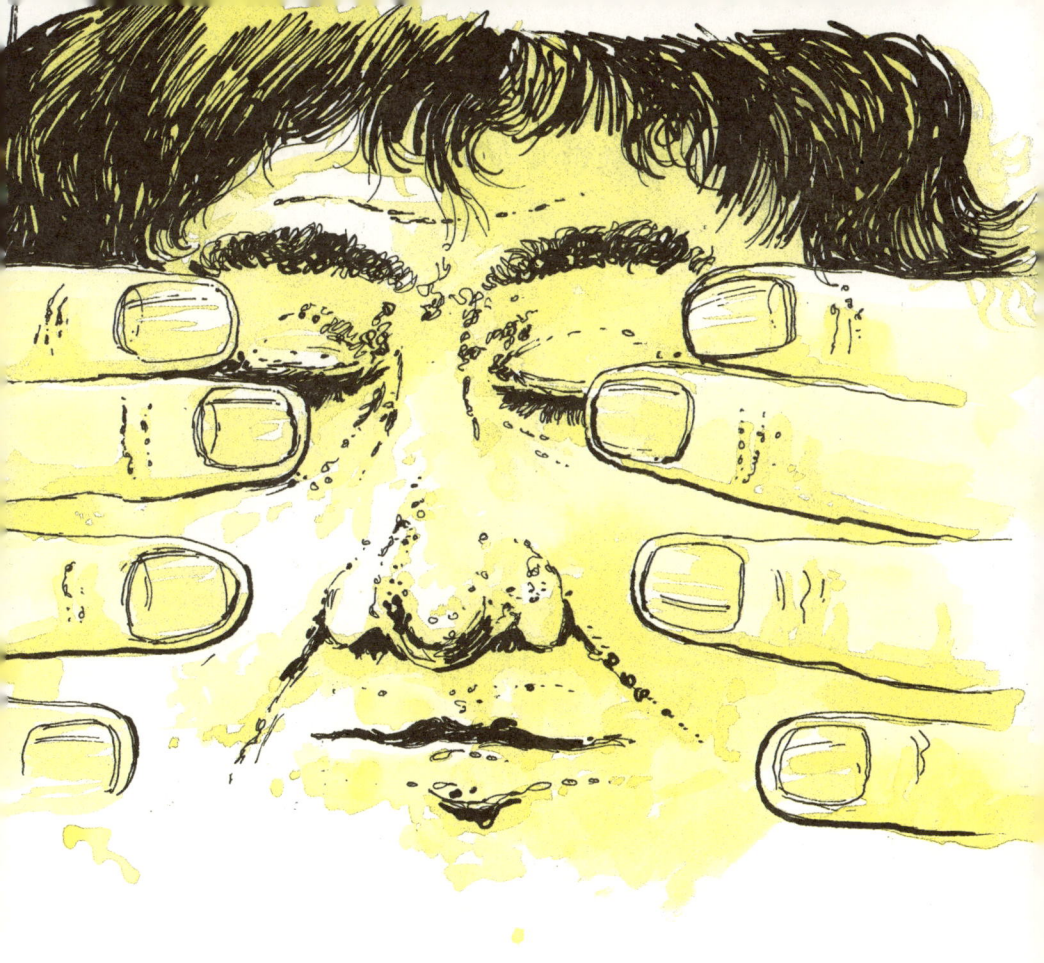

The meeting with Jesus had completely changed
Paul's life. He had been fighting against Jesus. Now he
knew that Jesus really was God's Son. Paul was
ashamed of what he had done. From now on his life
belonged to Jesus.

Paul went to the Jewish synagogues and began to
tell everyone the good news about Jesus. People
couldn't believe he was the same man!

Before long the Jews were planning to kill Paul. But
one dark night his friends lowered him from the city
wall in a basket—and Paul escaped. He went straight to
Jerusalem to join the friends of Jesus.

Peter and Cornelius

Peter was visiting the scattered groups of Christians.
They loved to hear him talk about Jesus. At Joppa,
Peter stayed with a leather-worker called Simon, in a
house by the sea.

A few miles away, at Caesarea, Cornelius had his
house. He was a soldier in the Roman army—a captain
in the Italian Regiment. Cornelius admired the Jews,
and their God. How different he was from the gods of
Rome! Cornelius did all he could to help the poor. And
he said his prayers every day. But he wasn't a Jew. He
could never hope to be one of God's people.

Then, one afternoon, an angel came to him:

'God has heard your prayers,' he said. 'There is a
man called Peter staying at Joppa. Send for him. He has
something God wants you to hear.' And he told
Cornelius where Peter was staying.

At noon the next day, Peter was on the flat roof of
Simon's house, praying. He was glad of the shade of the
big awning. He could smell the food cooking and he felt
hungry. His eyes closed . . .

. . . Someone was letting down a big sheet. It was
held, like the awning, by the corners. In it were all
kinds of creatures—birds and animals. Some of them
were on the list of 'unclean' foods that no Jew would
eat. God's law forbade it.

'Get up, Peter,' said a voice. 'Kill and eat.'

'I can't do that. Those creatures are unclean.'

'Don't say anything is unclean, if God says it is
clean.'

Three times this happened. And Peter knew that his

dream was a message from God. But what did it mean?

At that moment Cornelius's men knocked at the door. When Peter met Cornelius, he understood God's message. The good news about Jesus wasn't just for the Jews. It was for everyone.

Cornelius had invited all his friends and neighbours to hear Peter speak.

'It doesn't matter what country you come from,' Peter said. 'God treats everyone alike.' And he told them all about Jesus.

When Peter had finished, God sent his Spirit. It was like the Day of Pentecost all over again.

Not long after this King Herod Agrippa (grandson of King Herod the Great) arrested James and had him executed. The Christians were praying hard for Peter, who was in prison too. There was no hope of escape. His hands were chained, and he slept between two guards.

But in the night, God's angel came to Peter's cell and woke him up. The chains fell from his wrists.

'Fasten your belt. Put on your coat and shoes, and come with me,' the angel said.

Peter thought he was dreaming!

They passed the guards at their posts. Now they were at the gate. It opened for them and they went through. Peter found himself in the street outside. There was no sign of the angel. A cool breeze made him shiver.

'It's really true!' he thought. 'God sent his angel to rescue me!' And he hurried to the house of Mary, the mother of John Mark.

The Christians were all inside, praying.

Peter knocked at the door.

A servant girl called Rhoda answered it. She recognized Peter's voice—and ran back in to tell the others, leaving him standing outside.

At first they thought she was crazy. But the knocking went on, and at last they opened the door, and Peter told them his story.

At the prison, next morning, no one could work out what had happened—least of all the unhappy guards. And when no one could find Peter, Herod had the guards put to death.

The travels of Paul

At Antioch in Syria more and more people were becoming Christians. They needed teachers. Barnabas came from Jerusalem to help. And he fetched Paul, who had gone home to Tarsus.

But God had other work for these two men to do.

'I need Barnabas and Paul for a special job,' he told the leaders of the church. 'They must go to the people who have never heard of Jesus.'

They went first to Cyprus, where Barnabas was born. The island governor made them welcome. He listened to all they had to say. And he became a follower of Jesus. It was a good beginning.

Another sea voyage took them to Turkey. There they travelled overland—mostly on foot—from town to town.

They always went to the synagogues first, to tell the Jews. But few of them would listen. They refused to believe that Jesus was God's promised King. Often they stirred up trouble. Paul and Barnabas had some narrow escapes.

But in every town some people were eager to listen and put their trust in Jesus. Paul and Barnabas chose leaders for each new Christian group before they moved on.

Back at Antioch again, they told the Christians all 'that had happened. Before long Paul was off on his travels again. This time he took Silas with him. They went overland to Lystra in Turkey, where they were joined by a young man called Timothy. They reached the coast, and Paul was wondering where to go next, when he had a dream. A man from Greece was calling out to him:

'Come to Greece and help us!'

When he woke up, Paul was certain this was a message from God. So they set sail across the Aegean Sea.

In jail at Philippi

About a week later, Paul and Silas were in a Greek jail! They had been arrested at Philippi and flogged. (This was against the law, for Paul was not only a Jew, he was also a Roman citizen, with special rights. But the Philippians did not know this.)

In the jail, at midnight, Paul and Silas were praying to God and singing hymns. Their backs were so sore they could not sleep. Suddenly they felt the shock of an earthquake. The prison doors stood open. The prisoners' chains fell off.

The jailer thought they had all escaped. He would have killed himself if Paul had not shouted out. Instead, he became a Christian! By the time Paul and his friends left Philippi, there was a little group of Christians there.

Paul began to write letters to keep in touch with them, and with the other Christian groups. His letters were full of concern and practical help—as well as teaching about Jesus.

Athens and Corinth

From Philippi Paul and his friends travelled south. When Paul reached Athens he was upset to find this great city full of idols. The Parthenon, the temples and the market-place were beautiful buildings. But the people knew nothing about the one, true God. He began at once to tell them about him—and about Jesus and his resurrection.

The Athenians were great debaters. Paul was called before the city council, so that they could hear this new teaching. They enjoyed the debate, but not many people became Christians in Athens.

So Paul went on to the bustling city of Corinth. He made two new friends there: a Jew called Aquila and his wife Priscilla. Paul stayed with them and earned his living making tents, as they did. For eighteen months Paul and his friends taught the people of Corinth about Jesus.

Riot at Ephesus

They all set sail together: Aquila and Priscilla for
Ephesus; Paul and his friends for Antioch. Before long,
Paul was in Ephesus too. He stayed there for two years,
teaching.

Ephesus was famous for its temple to the goddess
Diana. The silversmiths grew rich by selling small
silver images of the goddess. But thanks to Paul and his
friends, so many people became Christians that their
sales fell.

Demetrius, one of the silversmiths, stirred up a
furious crowd. There was a riot! Two of Paul's friends
were dragged to the great open-air theatre. The crowd
stayed there shouting and screaming for hours, until
the town clerk managed to calm them down.

When things were quiet, Paul called the Christians
together and said goodbye. He went back to Greece
first, and then set sail for Jerusalem.

He knew there was danger ahead. So when his ship
called in at a port near Ephesus, he sent for his friends.
Paul encouraged them, and they prayed together. Then,
sadly, they went with him to the ship and watched
it sail away.

Prison—and shipwreck

Before he had been in Jerusalem long, Paul was in the middle of another riot! The Jews thought he had taken a non-Jewish friend into the Temple. (This was strictly forbidden.) Roman soldiers arrived just in time to save Paul's life.

Even in prison Paul was not safe. There was a plot against him, and he had to be moved to Caesarea. There the Jews brought their charges against him, and the Roman governor, Felix, heard Paul's defence. But he made no judgement. Two years later, when Festus replaced Felix as governor, Paul was still in prison.

'Are you willing to go to Jerusalem for trial?' he asked.

Paul was a Roman citizen. He had the right to put his case to the Emperor.

'No,' he said. 'I appeal to the Emperor.'

'Then I will send you to Rome,' Festus said.

It was late September when they set sail. Julius, a Roman officer in the Emperor's regiment, was in charge of Paul and some other prisoners. Off Crete, the ship ran into a gale. It was impossible to hold the course. So they took down the sail and ran before the wind. Next day they threw some of the cargo overboard to lighten the ship. The storm raged for fourteen days.

They could not see the sun, or the stars. So they did
not know where they were.

Then one night the sailors sensed that they were
close to land. Afraid of smashing on the rocks, they put
out all their anchors. At dawn Paul encouraged them
all to eat some food.

'The ship will be lost,' he said. 'But God has
promised to save all our lives.'

When day came the ship ran aground on a
sandbank and began to break up. The soldiers wanted
to kill the prisoners, but Julius would not let them. He
wanted to save Paul's life. He ordered those who could
swim to make for the land. The rest were to follow,
holding on to planks of wood. And so everyone got
safely ashore. They learnt, then, that they were on the
island of Malta!

There was no thought of sailing again until Spring.
This time all went well. And so Paul came to Rome.

The Christians came out to meet him. For the next
two years, while he waited for trial, Paul welcomed all
who came to see him. And he taught them about the
Lord Jesus Christ.

The good news had spread from Jerusalem. It had been
carried to Antioch in Syria, to Greece and Rome. All

over the Roman Empire Christians were sharing the message of Jesus with their friends. Like Paul, they were ready to suffer and die for their faith.

What happened after this is another story—one that covers 2,000 years and the whole world. It has not ended yet. But it will end when Jesus comes again. Then there will be a new heaven and a new earth, and God will live with his people for ever.